"Tyler has a brilliant way with words—taking insight from the bar side as well as from a world traveler and writer's perspective—and in *Tiny Cocktails* he manages to channel the cocktail world's enthusiasm and marries it with a practicality that many home bartenders won't have considered. Not only do these amazing recipes and anecdotes give an insight into some wonderful flavors and combinations, they also offer a window into a bartender's love of their craft and creating unique (mini) experiences in any setting."

—RYAN CHETIYAWARDANA,
award-winning bartender and founder of Mr Lyan

"Tyler has, once again, gone behind the scenes with some of the world's best bartenders to help us all drink better at home. *Tiny Cocktails* offers a fresh perspective on entertaining that is both practical and full of insider tips. It will be my dinner party companion for years to come."

—TALIA BAIOCCHI,
founder and editor in chief, Punch

TINY
COCKTAILS

TINY COCKTAILS

THE ART OF MINIATURE MIXOLOGY

by **TYLER ZIELINSKI**

Photographs by **ERIC MEDSKER**

CLARKSON POTTER/PUBLISHERS
New York

CONTENTS

29 → AMUSE-BOUCHES

NIGHTCAPS

LITTLE LUXURIES

INTRODUCTION

THE FEELING OF DRINKING A COCKTAIL—the sophistication of the glass in your hand and the resulting buzz that consumes you after a few rounds—is one undeniably significant element of the cocktail experience. But as empowering as it may feel to put on your best James Bond or Marilyn Monroe impression as you swiftly see off an ice-cold martini built to your precise specifications, it's easy to allow this single aspect of the drinking experience to overshadow the profundity of a cocktail's flavor. I believe neglecting to appreciate the spectrum of what a cocktail offers is where most imbibers sell themselves short.

As I've traveled to visit some of the world's best cocktail bars, I've had the privilege of tasting some extraordinary flavors and ingredients, becoming an insatiable flavor hunter in the process. But, as I've been reminded time and time again on my booze-filled excursions, there's one unfortunate hurdle that we all face while drinking cocktails: the human body's inability to handle the volume of liquid and alcohol that an unquenchable thirst for flavor demands.

The solution to this first-world problem? Tiny cocktails.

These miniature versions of beloved classic cocktails, or original creations designed to be enjoyed in a smaller format, nudged their way into mainstream cocktail culture after being unintentionally imagined, and subsequently championed, into existence by bartenders in the 2010s as a cheeky "bartender's handshake." Often created on the spur of the moment by mercurial bartenders (see the history of the Snaquiri, page 57), these small-format serves have evolved into a legitimate beverage offering at many cutting-edge bars around the world.

Luckily for us cocktail-inclined epicures, the tiny cocktail's timely ascent to popularity gives us the opportunity to experience a greater variety of flavors without the unnecessary overindulgence. In a way, they're the cocktail equivalent of tapas—a chance to taste lots, if you'd like, without suffering the inevitable consequences of putting too much booze in your body.

To appreciate the art of the cocktail is to enjoy the spectrum of what it offers from the first sip to the last: the aroma and taste, the sensation of a chilled glass on your lips, and the nuanced flavor of the liquid washing over your tongue. But equally as salient are the conversations and memorable moments that fill the drinking session from glass full to glass empty, and the stories of history and culture that exist in each luxurious libation. These impactful, flavor-led experiences possess the potential to change the way we think about cocktails. And, in rarer circumstances, redirect our life path, as was the case with me and one mushroom-filled cocktail back in 2014 (see The Cambridge on page 85 for more on that experience).

In *Tiny Cocktails*, you'll quickly learn, as I have, that sometimes less is more. Larger volume doesn't equate to superior flavor, or an optimal drinking experience. There are many cases where a cocktail is extraordinarily delicious for the first few sips, only to then decrease in desirability for a

variety of reasons: Maybe it's too rich or bold for a full serving (for example, drinks with cream, egg, or big flavors, like smoke); or it is best enjoyed while ice-cold and needs to be drunk sooner rather than later.

To make it easy to navigate the recipes in this book, I've divided the cocktail chapters into a few drinking occasions. There are the "Amuse-Bouches," an array of cocktails ideal for kicking off an evening; the "Nightcaps," a selection of cocktails perfect to have after dinner or at the end of the evening; and the "Little Luxuries," a range of upscale libations made with rare and more complex ingredients, which are best used in small quantities on special occasions.

Interspersed among these chapters is an array of curated recipes from some of the world's most highly regarded bartenders, who I've had the privilege of becoming acquainted with over the years. Many of them differ in style from the cocktails I created for this book. Such is the case with Aidan Bowie's Razz Baby (see page 33), a fizzy aperitif that calls for an intricate raspberry shrub laced with cacao nibs and rose water—a combination that is more representative of Bowie's preferred flavor palette than my own. I believe these differences are important because they highlight the breadth and depth of tiny cocktails and accurately reflect how they're showing up in cocktail culture today.

Throughout the book there are some custom ingredients, such as syrups and infusions, that will enhance your cocktails. I've made sure that minimal equipment and tools are required, so don't fret; you won't need a centrifuge or refractometer, or anything too high-tech. All you'll need is a well-stocked home bar and pantry and some basic tools to get started (see pages 11 and 19).

Most important is the glassware (see page 24), to which I've dedicated some space. Arguably the most difficult part of crafting tiny cocktails is sourcing the correctly sized glassware to accommodate the pared-back recipes. I've shared some tips for the best places to buy tiny rocks glasses, coupes, martini glasses, and highballs, so you can serve and enjoy your tiny tipples with panache. Chances are that you probably have an appropriately sized vessel or two lying around the house already.

Tiny Cocktails is an appreciation, as well as an exploration, of flavor. There's a time and place for the standard-sized cocktail, of course, but this book champions the act of savoring the flavor of every last fleeting drop of liquid from a cocktail that you never want to end. After a number of tiny cocktails, you may still feel that gleeful buzz and find yourself unleashing an unsolicited performance of "Sweet Caroline," or some other mainstream banger. But at least you'll have mindfully enjoyed more flavor in the process.

By the time you finish working your way through *Tiny Cocktails*, you'll have refined your bartending skills to the point where you'll be ready for the most complex at-home cocktail recipes. You may not end up tossing tins and bottles around like Tom Cruise in *Cocktail*, but you'll sure as hell be able to make a damn good martini.

Whether you reference this book for the tiny, yet insightful, bartender-caliber cocktails—big and bold drinks that lend themselves to micro sizes—or simply for creative inspiration to develop your own original tiny serve, my hope is that you discover a newfound appreciation for not only the flavor but also the art of the tiny cocktail.

STRAINER

COCKTAIL SHAKERS

MEASURES

GRATER

BAR SPOON

MISE EN PLACE

Mise en place is a French culinary phrase that's regularly used in kitchens and bars. It means "putting in place" and refers to the preparation required before cooking or mixing drinks. It's used in a variety of ways, from the efficiency-driven organization of tools and equipment within a bar or kitchen station to ensuring all ingredients are stocked and prepared for service. In essence, mise en place is about the preparation done to effectively and efficiently complete the task at hand.

As it relates to mixing drinks, mise en place includes stocking and sorting glassware, bar tools, ice, garnishes, cocktail ingredients, and so on. This section is designed to ensure you have everything you need to make the recipes in this book.

TOOLS OF THE TRADE

Fundamentally, mixing drinks is as much a science as it is an art. And just as scientists need their beakers, microscopes, and other, more sophisticated tools of measurement to successfully do their jobs, bartenders also need proper mixing tools in order to craft well-balanced cocktails.

Thankfully, you don't need tons of items to complete your basic home-bartending setup, and most of the tools required are pretty affordable. Like most things, though, you get what you pay for. To help you make the best selections for your bartending arsenal, I've curated the must-have tools for mixing cocktails, along with some recommended brands. Let the mise en place begin.

BAR SPOON

Required for stirring and layering ingredients, the bar spoon is an essential tool of the trade. As for which spoon to pick, it's very much a case of preference. Bar spoons come in a variety of lengths and styles—some have fork-shaped tips for picking brandied cherries, while others resemble a teardrop or have a small circle used for efficient layering of ingredients. The shape of the spoon itself, though, is the most important detail. The standard bowl of a bar spoon should hold about ⅛ ounce, or ¾ teaspoon, of liquid. The "barspoon" is a common measurement, which you'll find in recipes throughout this book, given the micro-sized drink recipes. So for accuracy and consistency, it's important to get a bar spoon with this capacity. Thankfully, all of the ones sold on Cocktail Kingdom are built to this specification.

BLENDER

The blender has gone in and out of fashion over the past century. Today, blenders are used sparingly behind bars, with the exception of tiki and tropical bars, where frozen drinks are commonly served. But since cocktail ingredient preparations have become more sophisticated over the past two decades, the blender has found other uses in the back of house, where it's mostly used to prepare syrups and spirit infusions.

In this book, there aren't any blended cocktails, but there are some ingredient preparations that require blending. A small personal blender will suffice, but a full-sized one is best. Ninja and Vitamix brands are the ones worth investing in—they'll go the distance.

BOTTLES

For batches of liquid ingredients, such as custom syrups, cordials, and infusions, you'll need some bottles to decant into. A US brand that home bartenders have really taken to is Crew Supply Co., because the bottles come in a few sizes and the bottoms can be screwed off, which makes for easy cleaning and filling. The Chubby bottle, which holds about 15 ounces, is my personal favorite, as I rarely prepare large batches of ingredients at home to avoid wastage. But the brand also sells larger bottles should those suit your fancy. Of course, you can save random jars and bottles, including liquor bottles, but make sure to use vessels that can be mostly filled up by the liquid stored inside, and are sanitized before usage. Oxygen is not your friend when it comes to storing liquid ingredients in bottles, especially nonalcoholic ones, which can spoil more quickly when exposed to oxygen.

Filling up your bottles will give the contents a longer shelf life.

CLEAR ICE MOLDS

The ingredient that most cocktail lovers overlook is water. On average, the water content of the cocktails we drink is anywhere between 25 and 30 percent of their total volume, and all of that water comes from the ice used to chill and dilute it. Therefore, the quality of the ice we serve our cocktails over, and the ice we mix with, matters. Most cocktails benefit from the sustained chill, slower rate of dilution, and purity of the water content that clear ice lends to drinks. For smaller drinks, clear ice is a simple way to improve the aesthetics of the drink and keep the overall quality high, even as the ice melts. Many brands have entered the market in the last decade, but Ghost Ice, Wintersmiths, and True Cubes have stolen the hearts of professional and home bartenders alike, so they're the ones worth adding to your home bar.

COCKTAIL SHAKER

The cocktail shaker's main purpose is to combine ice and a mix of ingredients through vigorous agitation, creating one cohesive drink that's properly aerated, chilled, and diluted.

Shakers come in a variety of shapes, sizes, and styles, but the easiest way to categorize them is by two-piece shakers, which come in three styles: tin-on-tin or glass-on-tin shakers, known as the Boston shaker, and the less common Parisian shaker; and the three-piece shaker, best known as the cobbler shaker.

There are subtle nuances between these shakers and how they impact a cocktail, based on the shaker's shape, size, and what it's made from. For the purposes of this book, though, any shaker will do. My recommendation is to buy a two-piece tin-on-tin number. They're durable and easy to work with and source. Cocktail Kingdom's Kariko weighted shaking tin set is the industry standard and goes the distance without costing a ton. If you love the idea of mixing with a stylish three-piece cobbler shaker to practice your hard shake, that will also suffice.

FILTERS

When making clarified milk punches (see Milking It, page 119), cordials, or infusions containing superfine particles—such as fruits or herbs that have been blended, or fat-washed spirits (see page 21)—you can strain these ingredients through a conical coffee filter, superbag, or cheesecloth. Just fit the coffee filter into a funnel or line a fine-mesh strainer with cheesecloth for double filtration.

ICE PICK

The ice pick is an essential tool to shape larger blocks or chunks of ice, or separate ice that's stuck together. For the purposes of mixing tiny drinks, an ice pick comes in handy for breaking down large clear cubes into smaller chunks that will fit into the glassware. Ice picks come in a couple of shapes and sizes, but I enjoy the three-spike (pitchfork) pick best.

JUICERS

Juicers really run the gamut. For at-home use in small volumes, a handheld citrus juicer (also known as a Mexican elbow citrus press) for lemons and limes will suffice most of the time. It's a way of juicing that incorporates more of the citrus peel's aromatic essential oils into the juice, too.

But ever since I had to manually juice enough citrus fruit to get about two gallons of juice before service as a young barback, I swore I'd never make any of my staff do the same on a large scale, and neither should you. Breville makes a sleek and efficient electric juicer that will go the distance, and SMEG sells one worth splurging on.

If you really want to level up your home bar and expand the ingredients you are working with, I'd strongly recommend a cold press juicer, such as the Hamilton or Ninja brands, for fresh fruit and vegetable juices. This appliance, which retains the juice's nutritional value and freshness, will easily transform cocktails like the Seafire Colada (page 97) from average to extraordinary and is worth splashing the cash for.

KITCHEN SCALE

In American households, a kitchen scale is, unfortunately, a rarity. It wasn't until I worked in bars and restaurants that I truly appreciated its value and necessity. Why is it so great, you may be wondering. Simply put, the weight of an ingredient is a more accurate measure than its volume. This can be attributed to an array of factors, including inconsistencies in the sizes and shapes of solid ingredients. But for the purposes of this book, all you need to know is that if you want a more balanced syrup or cordial, then weighing the ingredients instead of using cups or liquid ounces is the way to go. Should you decide to purchase a kitchen scale, KitchenAid and OXO are reliable brands to consider.

HARD SHAKE

The hard shake, typically performed with a cobbler shaker, is a shaking style that was introduced to cocktail culture by renowned Japanese bartender Kazuo Uyeda, the proprietor of Tender Bar in Tokyo's Ginza district. Instead of simply shaking back and forth like an engine's piston, this technique requires a bit more finesse.

This unique shake is defined by its signature three-point motion, starting with a wrist-snapping first shake at face level, then neck level, followed by chest level. The shake, which you should absolutely look up on YouTube to see in action, is thought to yield better aeration and texture in cocktails, with the rhythmic back-and-forth movement allowing the ice within the shaker to roll in a figure-eight motion instead of getting smashed from end to end, which adds more dilution. It's more technique driven than the standard shake, but it's one that might be fun to learn if you want to up your home bartending game.

MEASURES

A jigger is what most cocktail bartenders use to measure liquid ingredients into a shaker or mixing glass instead of free pouring. There are a range of jiggers, which come in all shapes and sizes. But for tiny cocktails, given the tiny measures, you'll want to purchase a ½-ounce and ¾-ounce jigger and a 1-ounce and 1½-ounce jigger, as they'll be most relevant for the cocktails mixed in this book. There are many types of jiggers available, but here are two that I recommend for tiny cocktails in particular:

The Japanese jigger is one of the most popular among cocktail bartenders because it's easy to handle, and its long, slender shape minimizes the margin for error in over- or under-pouring. Most important, in this style, you can buy the appropriately sized jigger for smaller pours.

Stepped, graduated jiggers (similar to a tiny measuring cup) are great for novice home bartenders because all the measurements are in one cup and are easily read. The clear OXO jigger, in particular, is one many bartenders swear by because you can read the measurements from the outside of the jigger and from the top down, and you can measure in both ounces and milliliters.

Teaspoons and tablespoons can also be used to measure tiny cocktails, but you'll have to do the tedious work of translating the measurements from ounces. To start: 1½ teaspoons equals ¼ ounce; 1 tablespoon equals ½ ounce; and 2 tablespoons equals 1 ounce.

MICROPLANE

Admittedly, a cheese grater can do the job of a Microplane, but it lacks the finesse of this simple grating tool. A Microplane is ideal for garnishing a sour cocktail with fine citrus zest, a cream-topped cocktail with fresh nutmeg, or an indulgent nightcap with morsels of dark chocolate.

MILK FROTHER

Today, many bars use a milk frother instead of dry shaking (without ice) drinks that call for egg white. This book doesn't include any egg white cocktails, as I believe they're better suited for standard-size drinks. But the milk frother can be used to aerate the Tropical Garibaldi (page 39), or shaken cocktails that are served up, such as the Snaquiri (page 57), by aerating the mix in the tin before adding ice and shaking to chill and dilute it. It's a tool worth having on hand, even if it's only used occasionally.

MIXING GLASS

While some bartenders still use a pint glass or shaking tin to stir cocktails, it's best to have a mixing glass. Why?

A well-designed mixing glass has a wider base than an average pint glass or shaking tin, which tend to taper toward the base. This means that, on average, a mixing glass can comfortably fit four 1-inch ice cubes at the base of the glass, while a pint glass or shaking tin can only fit a couple. The wider base maximizes the liquid-ice contact throughout the mixing glass, for a better chilled and diluted cocktail.

But wait, things get even nerdier! Mixing glasses can be either metal or glass, and while the glass option is my personal go-to for aesthetic purposes, the metal ones are more durable and perform better. Compared to glass, metal, which is a better conductor of thermal energy, creates a more consistent temperature when mixing. This feat gives the bartender more control over a cocktail's temperature and dilution when mixing (note: the temperature of a cocktail directly correlates to the volume of dilution). The differences in cocktail quality when mixing with metal versus glass are minuscule, but worth mentioning, as I believe it's important to understand why bartenders choose one type instead of the other.

MUDDLER

Of all of the bar tools, I'd say the muddler is the one that's most optional and more of a nice-to-have. A wooden spoon can muddle any ingredients necessary, but if you want a more aesthetic choice, there are plenty of great options to choose from.

PARING KNIFE AND CUTTING BOARD

For slicing citrus fruit into wheels, and trimming pineapple leaves and other unruly garnishes, a sharp paring knife and a cutting board are essential for anyone mixing drinks. If you've yet to acquire these essentials, then pop by your local home goods store or buy them online.

STRAINERS

If you're using a cobbler shaker, which already has a built-in strainer, you won't need a Hawthorne or julep strainer to strain the cocktail. But if you're using a two-piece shaker, a Hawthorne strainer will make sure the ice you use to chill and dilute your cocktail remains in the shaker.

The other strainer worth purchasing is a small fine-mesh strainer (OXO is my preferred brand). To ensure no ice chips or unwanted bits of pulp or other particles are left floating in your cocktail, strain the drink in the shaking tin through both a Hawthorne strainer and a fine-mesh strainer. Known as double straining, this is standard practice at most cocktail bars for drinks that contain eggs, herbs, and ingredients that need to be more diligently filtered.

Y PEELER

The Y peeler is an essential tool for cutting citrus peels. My favorite brand, again, is OXO, because their Y peeler fits comfortably in the hand and has a rubber grip to ensure your citrus juice—covered hands don't slide all over the place. But first, be sure to watch a

YouTube video on how to properly use one to avoid injury. You may be laughing now, because it is semi-comical, but losing part of a fingertip happens more often than you'd think.

STOCKING THE PANTRY

A pantry that's well stocked with essentials is a gateway to infinite flavor possibilities. The more ingredients you have on hand—even cheffy items such as tahini or miso (see the Miso-Honey Syrup in the Miso Gold Rush, page 77)—the easier it will be for you to craft bespoke cocktails.

Just as cocktail bars stock their pantries with ingredients required to create daily essentials—syrups, cordials, and infusions—you should do the same (just on a smaller scale).

While there are some universal items that every home bar needs, such as sweeteners for syrups and citrus fruit for popular classic cocktails, there is no one-size-fits-all list; people's cocktail pantries are subjective and reflect their flavor preferences. Don't like shaken citrus cocktails? Then you probably don't need to stock up on citrus fruit, aside from the odd orange or lemon for citrus peel garnishes. Not a fan of Tommy's margarita–style drinks? Then you can probably pass on the agave nectar, too.

The checklist below is by no means a comprehensive list of everything you'll need for the drink recipes that follow. But these essentials will guarantee that you will, at the bare minimum, be able to make tiny versions of the classic-inspired cocktails I've included, while also giving you foundational ingredients for coming up with your own variations once you've mastered all of the tiny cocktail recipes.

SWEETENERS

- ☐ Agave nectar
- ☐ Demerara sugar
- ☐ Granulated white sugar
- ☐ Honey

CANNED AND BOTTLED ITEMS

- ☐ Coconut cream, preferably Coco Lopez
- ☐ Coconut milk
- ☐ Pineapple juice
- ☐ Verjus

TEAS AND TISANES

- ☐ Chamomile tisane
- ☐ Earl Grey tea
- ☐ English Breakfast tea
- ☐ Hibiscus tisane

FATS

- ☐ Almond butter
- ☐ Coconut oil
- ☐ Extra-virgin olive oil
- ☐ Ghee
- ☐ Tahini
- ☐ Unsalted butter

COFFEE

ACID POWDERS

- ☐ Ascorbic acid powder
- ☐ Citric acid powder
- ☐ Malic acid powder

ACID POWDERS

These may seem intimidating if you've never used them before, but they've become an essential ingredient in the modern bartender's pantry. Aside from making cocktail ingredients more acidic, acid powders, especially ascorbic and citric acid, can also act as a preservative. Ascorbic, citric, and malic acid powders are the primary ones you'll need for this book, but lactic and tartaric acids are also fun to play around with if you decide to develop your own creations.

OLIVES

- ☐ Castelvetrano olives (pitted)
- ☐ Kalamata olives (pitted)

CITRUS FRUITS

- ☐ Grapefruit
- ☐ Lemon
- ☐ Lime
- ☐ Orange

HERBS AND SPICES

- ☐ Basil (fresh)
- ☐ Cinnamon (ground and sticks)
- ☐ Mint (fresh)
- ☐ Nutmeg (ground and whole)
- ☐ Sea salt (fine)

DAIRY PRODUCTS

- ☐ Heavy cream
- ☐ Milk

NUTS AND SEEDS

- ☐ Almonds
- ☐ Sunflower seeds

SPARKLING WINE

HOW TO FAT-WASH A SPIRIT

Fat-washing is a type of infusion whereby a fatty ingredient, such as an oil or butter, imparts flavor, body, and mouthfeel to a spirit through a multi-step process that I explain in further detail below. It was introduced to cocktail culture in 2007 by the bartending legend Don Lee, who was working at New York's pioneering speakeasy-style bar, PDT, at the time. The result of his innovation was the famous Benton's Old-Fashioned, made with an indulgent Benton's bacon fat–washed whiskey, maple syrup, and Angostura bitters. To fat-wash your own spirit, first combine the fat with the desired spirit (e.g. olive oil and vodka). If the fat is an oil that is liquid at room temperature, combine it with the spirit in a container or zip seal bag (make sure you remove all the air) and infuse at room temperature for a minimum of 4 hours, but up to 12 hours. Or put the mixture in a warm-water bath for a few hours. The time will vary, depending on the intensity of the fat flavor, and if heat is added, which accelerates the infusion process.

If the fat is solid at room temperature, such as coconut oil, it will need heat to render to fully mix with the spirit and enhance the flavor that's extracted. At home, the best way to do this is to heat some water in a saucepan—fill it enough to cover more than half the infusion—until it is 120° to 150°F (below a simmer). Combine the fat and spirit in a ziplock bag or mason jar and place it in the heated water. Let it rest in the water bath for 4 hours, reheating the water bath every 30 minutes or so as it cools. (Note: If you have an immersion circulator, also known as sous vide, you can set the water bath to around 150°F—the temperature can range depending on the ingredients—and follow the same instructions for infusion time.)

Once you're done infusing the spirit, allow it to cool to room temperature, then put the bag or jar in the freezer overnight so the fat solidifies. Then strain the infusion through a fine-mesh strainer lined with a coffee filter before bottling. Fat-washed ingredients are best used within 1 to 2 months for optimal flavor. It's also worth noting that if you use animal fats to fat-wash a spirit, such as the bacon fat–washed rum in the HG Walter Old-Fashioned (page 89), it should be stored in the refrigerator for food safety purposes, where it will keep for up to 2 weeks.

ESSENTIAL SYRUPS

There are a few syrups that are essential to a bar service. And at home, even if you don't always have these syrups pre-made and refrigerated, I recommend having the ingredients on hand, ready to prepare at a moment's notice. For me, as you'll find at most cocktail bars, the essential three syrups are Simple Syrup, Honey Syrup, and Agave Syrup.

When making these syrups, measure by weight, if possible, for the sake of accuracy. But volume will suffice if you haven't been sold by my not-so-subtle nudge to buy a kitchen scale (see page 15).

SIMPLE SYRUP

1 PART GRANULATED SUGAR

1 PART FRESHLY BOILED WATER

In a heatproof container, combine the sugar and boiled water, and stir thoroughly to dissolve the sugar. If all the sugar hasn't dissolved and the water has cooled, microwave it for 20 to 30 seconds until it's hot again, and then stir to dissolve. Let cool to room temperature, and transfer to a bottle. Store, tightly sealed, in the refrigerator for up to 1 month.

NOTE: You can use this recipe template to make other sugar syrups, such as demerara, used in A Wee Irish Coffee (page 169). Simply substitute in demerara sugar, or another type of sugar, for the granulated sugar and proceed with the recipe as written. To make a rich simple syrup, mix 2 parts sugar to 1 part water.

HONEY SYRUP

2 PARTS HONEY

1 PART FRESHLY BOILED WATER

In a mason jar, combine the honey and boiled water, and stir thoroughly to blend. Let cool to room temperature, and pour into a bottle. Store, tightly sealed, in the refrigerator for up to 1 month.

NOTE: For a richer honey syrup, try 3 parts honey to 1 part water.

AGAVE SYRUP

2 PARTS AGAVE NECTAR

1 PART FRESHLY BOILED WATER

In a mason jar, combine the agave and boiled water, and stir thoroughly to blend. Let cool to room temperature, and pour into a bottle. Store, tightly sealed, in the refrigerator for up to 1 month.

GUIDE TO TINY GLASSWARE

The most challenging aspect of mixing tiny cocktails is sourcing the appropriately sized glassware to serve them in. You can mess up mixing a drink, use a mason jar instead of a cocktail shaker, and you can even make my Snaquiri (page 57) with an unbalanced simple syrup, if you didn't accurately measure the ratio of sugar to water. But serving any drink in a glass that's too big for it is an absolute no-no.

Just as the liquid components of the cocktail should be in harmony, so should the visual composition, which also includes ice and garnishes. The general rule is that a cocktail's vessel should never be uncomfortably empty (you'll know what I mean when you see it). The definition of "uncomfortably empty" can vary from cocktail to cocktail, but it'll typically look like your bartender forgot to finish filling your glass.

In general, for drinks served over ice (e.g., old-fashioneds) or in a wine glass, choose a vessel with a capacity between two and three times the size of your drink. So for a 2-ounce drink,

the vessel should hold between 4 and 5 ounces. For a drink that is traditionally served without ice (as opposed to one that can be served either way, on the rocks or up), choose a vessel with a capacity that is only about 1 ounce larger than the drink's volume (dilution included), or slightly less.

To ensure you're serving the most alluring tiny cocktails, I've provided guidance below on the ideal volume for each style of glassware—rocks, highball, coupe, and martini. And I've also recommended brands and models for you to consider. Some of these you may also already have at home. As long as your vessel—be it ceramic or glass— fits the specifications I've provided, your tiny cocktails are set to be executed in bartender-caliber fashion. The most important detail to remember: Always chill your glasses in the freezer for at least 30 minutes before serving your cocktail (for thicker glasses, which take longer to cool, chill for at least an hour). Trust me, once you do, you'll never go back.

TINY ROCKS GLASS

IDEAL VOLUME: 4½ to 7 ounces (or 130 to 200 ml)

If you have a hard time finding tumblers or rocks glasses this small, you may need to use more ice to fill the negative space. Unfortunately, there is no easy fix for a tiny cocktail served in a tiny rocks glass without ice, such as the Banana Bread (page 107). In fact, you'll need a glass on the smaller side of the volume range.

RECOMMENDED MODELS:

LSA Gio 7.4-ounce (220 ml) tumbler, lsa-international.com

Toyo-Sasaki 09105HS 5-ounce (150 ml) glass, toyo.sasaki.co.jp

TINY HIGHBALL GLASS

IDEAL VOLUME: 5 to 6½ ounces (or 150 to 190 ml)

Given the nature of tiny cocktails, there are very few drinks served with lengtheners, such as carbonated mixers or juices, to make tiny highballs, but there are a few that call for them (see the Tropical Garibaldi, page 39). I recommend looking at Japanese glassware producers, as that's where I've had the most luck finding the right size glass.

RECOMMENDED MODELS:

Kimura Glass Asia plain 5-ounce (150 ml) tumbler, kimuraglass.com

Toyo-Sasaki 08205HS 5-ounce (150 ml) beer glass, toyo.sasaki .co.jp

TINY COUPES AND MARTINI GLASSES

IDEAL VOLUME: 2½ to 3¾ ounces (75 to 110 ml)

These are the easiest small glasses to find in shops and online. Some recipes specify a tiny coupe instead of a martini glass, but they're interchangeable for all intents and purposes.

RECOMMENDED MODELS:

Leopold 3¾-ounce (110 ml) mini coupe or 3-ounce (90 ml) cordial cocktail glass, cocktailkingdom.com

Schott Zwiesel Bar Special Likor Bowl or Bar Special Liquor Bowl (depending on where you live)

TASTING GLASS

IDEAL VOLUME: 3½ to 6½ ounces (100 to 190 ml)

If you're a spirits aficionado, you likely already have one of these glasses, often sold as a "whisky" tasting glass, stocked at home. The shape of a tasting glass, which has a bulbous bowl and tapered rim, holds the liquid in a tighter space, which complements the structure of some drinks, such as the shape of the Seafire Colada's (page 97) fluffy head. It's also ideal for delicate spirit-forward drinks served up because they're designed to amplify a drink's aromatics, acting as a sufficient alternative to tiny coupes and martini glasses.

NOTE: While volumes of tasting glasses, such as the Glencairn, can have a liquid capacity of up to 6½ ounces, cocktails served in tasting glasses are typically only filled to just above the bowl.

RECOMMENDED MODELS:

Fontaine whisky & spirits glass, https://fontaineglass.com

6-ounce (175 ml) Glencairn tasting glass, 6½ ounce (190 ml) glass, glencairn.co.uk

SMALL WINE GLASS

IDEAL VOLUME: 4½ to 5 ounces (125 to 150 ml)

Vintage wine glasses from secondhand shops will almost always fit the bill in terms of size, and they are affordable and eclectic options. But there are good new models being made as well. Sometimes brands vary in whether they list the ideal volume to hold or the total capacity, so feel free to play around and if the smaller volume of these drinks looks good in the glass, go for it. Here are a couple of my favorites.

RECOMMENDED MODELS:

Richard Brendon wine glass, richardbrendon.com

Riedel ouverture white wine, riedel.com

CERAMICS

These textural works of art aren't an ideal fit for every cocktail. But I find ceramic cups particularly useful for hot drinks, or when a liquid mixture lacks visual appeal and needs the vessel to add a touch of panache. Because ceramic vessels vary in shape and size, look for those that are similar in shape and volume to the glassware specified.

For a hot drink served with a layer of cream, such as A Wee Irish Coffee (page 169), a tapered teacup or ceramic vessel that's 4 to 4½ ounces in volume (120 to 135 ml) is ideal. Note: Make sure the vessels you purchase are safe for serving food and alcohol.

RECOMMENDED MODELS:

Epalladio Art Workshop,
https://www.etsy.com/uk/shop/
EpalladioCeramics

Studio 1765's Obsession collection, www.studio1765.com/
obsession

MTC Kitchen,
www.mtckitchen.com

And don't forget to shop at your local ceramics studio or craft fair!

AMUSE-

When pioneering French chefs of the 1970s nouvelle cuisine movement introduced the amuse-bouche, a small bite served before the appetizer, to restaurant culture, it served one primary purpose: to stimulate the guest's appetite, preparing them for the robust meal ahead. In this chapter, the recipes I've developed as amuse-bouches serve a similar purpose. These drinks are meant to stimulate the appetite and palate with an array of fresh and uplifting flavors and textures. But they're also an ideal opportunity to give your company a strong first impression of your bartending skills, while kicking off an evening with a small dose of deliciousness.

While you can absolutely mix up some of these tiny tasters to enjoy on your own, the amuse-bouche is most in its element when provided as a hospitable gesture to others, similar to the way many of the world's best cocktail bars greet their guests with a welcome cocktail upon arrival.

There's a little something for every imbiber and every occasion here, and each recipe can be tweaked to your own liking as your mixology skills become more refined over time.

BOUCHES

RHUBARB CHAMPAGNE COCKTAIL

The sophisticated Champagne cocktail is an ideal welcome drink—it's simple, elegant, and easily customizable. It requires minimal effort for maximum satisfaction flavor (the home bartending dream). I ditch the classic sugar cube for a seasonal syrup flavored with one of spring's most beloved plants: rhubarb. This vibrant reddish-green vegetable is as pretty as it is delicious, boasting a balance of sweetness, acidity, and grassiness, which pairs beautifully with sparkling wine. Got a little time to spare and want to impress your dinner guests? Look no further than this mouthwatering amuse-bouche.

¼ OUNCE RHUBARB SYRUP 2 DASHES ANGOSTURA BITTERS SPLASH OF CHAMPAGNE	Pour the syrup into a chilled tiny coupe and add the bitters. Top with Champagne and serve.

RHUBARB SYRUP

MAKES ABOUT ½ CUP

½ CUP CHOPPED RHUBARB STEMS

½ CUP SUGAR

¼ CUP WATER

PINCH OF CITRIC ACID POWDER (OPTIONAL)

Combine the rhubarb stems, sugar, water, and citric acid powder (if using) in a saucepan over medium-low heat and cook until the rhubarb is tender and the sugar has dissolved, 3 to 5 minutes. Let the syrup cool to room temperature, and transfer it to a food processor or blender. Pulse until the rhubarb is pureed. Strain the mixture through a fine-mesh strainer lined with cheesecloth, and transfer to a bottle. Store, tightly sealed, in the refrigerator for up to 2 weeks.

PRO TIP: The shrub can also be mixed with soda water for a casual nonalcoholic drink.

RAZZ BABY

BY AIDAN BOWIE

THE DEAD RABBIT (NEW YORK CITY, WASHINGTON, D.C., AND AUSTIN, TEXAS)

For the Razz Baby, Aidan Bowie rolled back the years with a little gem of a taster from his days as head bartender at Dandelyan, a London bar that shuttered soon after being named the best bar in the world in 2018 by the World's 50 Best Bars.

"It could act like an amuse-bouche, but it's also great for celebrations and for people to finish their night on, too," Bowie says. The cocktail is simple in structure, yet complex in flavor, due to the sweet-and-sour house-made shrub. It's not often that cocktail lovers stumble across libations that graced the tables of the defunct Dandelyan, so this tiny tipple is a luxury worth savoring.

¼ OUNCE RASPBERRY SHRUB

DASH OF ABSINTHE

SPLASH OF CHAMPAGNE OR SPARKLING WINE

In a chilled tiny coupe, combine the shrub and absinthe. Top with Champagne, give a quick stir to mix, and enjoy.

→ RASPBERRY SHRUB

MAKES ABOUT ½ CUP

½ CUP FRESH RASPBERRIES

¼ CUP APPLE CIDER VINEGAR

¼ TEASPOON ROSE WATER

2 TABLESPOONS CACAO NIBS

½ TEASPOON SALT

SUPERFINE SUGAR

Combine the raspberries, vinegar, rose water, cacao nibs, and salt in a sanitized mason jar or other sealable vessel. Use a muddler to break down the raspberries. Let this mixture marry in the refrigerator for 2 to 4 days, stirring once each day. Strain the liquid through a fine-mesh strainer lined with cheesecloth. Measure the mixture in a measuring cup, or weigh it on a scale, and add half the volume (or weight) in sugar. Whisk to dissolve the sugar, transfer to a clean bottle, and store, tightly sealed, in the refrigerator for up to 6 months.

ART OF SIMPLICITY

Italicus, the shining star of this augmented Champagne cocktail, is an exquisite Italian aperitivo that I always stock at home, because the slightest dose of this aperitivo makes most drinks taste better. Cedro and bergamot—two types of citrus native to Italy—drive the powerful aromatic profile of this liqueur. And in the Art of Simplicity, the citrus is the star of the show. The Italicus is bolstered by a fragrant grapefruit sherbet—in this case a blend of the fruit's juice and the zest's oils—and lengthened with bubbly, the latter revealing the intricacies of this beloved liqueur as the carbonation brings the subtle floral notes to the surface. The sherbet recipe was developed by Agostino Perrone for his own cocktail contribution, Golden (page 67). It works beautifully in this amuse-bouche, which is designed to please the masses and is a pristine palate cleanser ideal before dinner or between the main course and dessert.

½ OUNCE ITALICUS ROSOLIO DI BERGAMOTTO LIQUEUR

¼ OUNCE GRAPEFRUIT SHERBET (PAGE 68)

SPLASH OF PROSECCO OR ANOTHER SPARKLING WINE

Garnish: 1 GREEN OLIVE, SUCH AS CASTELVETRANO, SKEWERED WITH A PICK

Combine the Italicus and sherbet in a chilled tiny coupe. Top with a splash of prosecco, garnish with the olive, and serve.

TOMATO & ELDERFLOWER SPRITZ

In both cooking and building cocktails, there are many foolproof flavor pairings that chefs and bartenders swear by. The nuanced savory-floral combination of tomato and elderflower is one of those tried-and-tested pairings. Each of them is robust—often sticking out like a sore thumb when used individually. But the marriage of tomato's long umami finish and elderflower's subtle tropical notes yields a flavor profile that's greater than the sum of its parts. In this spritz, you can use an array of complementary unaged spirits for the base. The cocktail is as customizable as it is lush, and will impress with minimal effort.

¾ OUNCE TEQUILA, GIN, OR VODKA

¼ OUNCE ELDERFLOWER LIQUEUR, PREFERABLY ST-GERMAIN

1 TEASPOON TOMATO SYRUP (PAGE 38)

¾ OUNCE SPARKLING WINE

¼ OUNCE SODA WATER

Garnish: 1 LEMON PEEL AND FREEZE-DRIED RASPBERRY POWDER

Wet half of the outer rim of a chilled tiny coupe or tasting glass and sprinkle with the raspberry powder, gently tapping the glass to knock off any excess and tidying with a napkin if necessary, so that you're left with a dusting. Combine the tequila, elderflower liqueur, Tomato Syrup, sparkling wine, and soda water in the chilled coupe or tasting glass. Express the lemon peel over the drink, discard, and enjoy the drink.

✳ BUILD A FLIGHT

If you're feeling ambitious, make three Tomato & Elderflower Spritzes, one with each of the recommended base spirits—tequila, gin, and vodka—and arrange in a flight.

CONTINUES

TOMATO SYRUP

MAKES ABOUT ¾ CUP

½ CUP CHERRY TOMATOES

¼ CUP WATER

½ TEASPOON SALT

4 FRESH CHOPPED BASIL STEMS

1 CUP GRANULATED SUGAR

PINCH OF CITRIC ACID POWDER (OPTIONAL; SEE NOTE)

NOTE: The citric acid powder bolsters the acidity and improves the shelf life of the syrup.

In a food processor, combine the tomatoes, water, salt, and basil stems and blend until the tomatoes and basil stems are pureed. Set a strainer lined with cheesecloth over a saucepan and pour the mixture through. Stir in the sugar and simmer over low heat, constantly stirring to avoid boiling, until the sugar has dissolved.

Remove from the heat and add a pinch of citric acid powder, if desired. Let the syrup cool to room temperature. Transfer to a bottle and refrigerate, tightly sealed, for up to 2 weeks. (Also try this syrup in place of Agave Syrup in the Pasilla Mixe Margarita, page 141, or the Fiesta on Warren, page 61.)

TROPICAL GARIBALDI

This homage to Dante's exceptional Garibaldi—a modern classic cocktail elevated to new heights at Caffe Dante in New York City—is the ideal drink to have if you are in dire need of some hair of the dog, or if you are looking for an easy-drinking brunch cocktail. The key to flawless execution is making sure the orange and pineapple juices are "fluffy," which is achieved here by aerating them together with a milk frother or hand blender. The Coconut Oil–Washed Campari is great to have on hand. Use it to change up the Shakerato (page 53) or spice up a Tiny Negroni (page 79).

1½ OUNCES FRESHLY SQUEEZED ORANGE JUICE

¾ OUNCE PINEAPPLE JUICE

¾ OUNCE COCONUT OIL–WASHED CAMPARI (PAGE 41; SEE NOTE)

Garnish: 1 SMALL PINEAPPLE LEAF

Combine the juices in a large cocktail tin and agitate with a milk frother or hand blender for 10 to 15 seconds to aerate. (Or, if you have one, use a high-speed juicer to extract and aerate the juices at the same time.) Put a small chunk of ice into a chilled tiny highball glass, and pour the Coconut Oil–Washed Campari over it. Top with the fluffy juice, gently agitate the mixture with a bar spoon to mix, and garnish with the pineapple leaf.

NOTE: If you don't have time to prepare the Coconut Oil–Washed Campari, you can achieve a similar flavor profile by substituting ½ ounce of Campari and ¼ ounce of coconut rum (such as Kōloa Kaua`i).

CONTINUES

COCONUT OIL-WASHED CAMPARI

MAKES ABOUT 5 OUNCES

6 OUNCES CAMPARI

2 OUNCES COCONUT OIL

Combine the Campari and coconut oil in a zip seal bag (making sure to remove all the air). Fill a saucepan with water and heat it to between 100° and 150°F (below a simmer). Remove the pan from the heat and put the bag in the water to melt the oil and infuse the Campari. Let it rest in the water bath for 4 hours, reheating the water every 30 minutes or so as it cools. (Alternatively, if you have an immersion circulator, cook sous vide at 120°F for the same length of time.) Freeze for 2 to 3 hours, until all the oil has solidified, and then strain the infused Campari through a coffee filter or a fine-mesh strainer lined with cheesecloth and transfer to a bottle. Store, tightly sealed, in the refrigerator and enjoy within 1 month for optimal freshness.

NOTE: Don't leave the infused Campari in the freezer for more than 3 hours, or its flavor will start to diminish and it is also at risk of freezing.

BROKEN SPANISH

BY **PIETRO COLLINA**

VIAJANTE 87 (LONDON)

 There are few bar operators as proficient and professional as Pietro Collina, a bartender whose résumé includes the NoMad hotels and the prestigious Eleven Madison Park. At almost all of the bars Collina has led over the years, he's always kept a few off-menu tiny serves, which he and his bar team would give to guests with their compliments or for a small price.

"I'd introduce them to guests who were having a good time, chatting with the bartenders, exploring the drinks," he said. The Broken Spanish, a drink created during his tenure at the since-shuttered NoMad in New York City, is a cocktail that Collina believes is ideal in a tiny format, as it retains its integrity and freshness from start to finish. After tasting a serve myself, I have to agree.

---

1 OUNCE FINO SHERRY (SUCH AS TIO PEPE)

¾ OUNCE VERJUS

¾ OUNCE COCCHI AMERICANO

¼ OUNCE BÉNÉDICTINE LIQUEUR

BECHEROVKA LIQUEUR FOR RINSING

Garnish: 1 GRAPEFRUIT TWIST

Combine the sherry, verjus, Cocchi Americano, and Bénédictine in a mixing glass filled with ice, and stir to chill and dilute. Rinse a chilled tiny coupe with Becherovka and dump out the excess (or drink it). Immediately strain the cocktail into the glass and garnish with the grapefruit twist.

LAZY PORN STAR

I came up with this playful deconstructed porn star martini for a guest-bartending shift that I did at Filthy XIII in Bristol, in the UK, in 2023.

The modern classic that inspired my serve was created at the Townhouse, in London, in 2003 by the late Douglas Ankrah. I reimagined it as a different sort of two-part drink: a small Champagne cocktail paired with a lethally delicious ice-cold shot of a layered vanilla vodka, which the Filthy XIII team helped me dial in.

I think cheeky cocktail names are great icebreakers, and this one did the trick. I'm still not sure if it was the name or the shot of vodka that made the atmosphere as buzzy as it was on that fine evening in Bristol, but either way it got the British seal of approval and that's enough for me.

½ OUNCE PASSION FRUIT
LIQUEUR (SUCH AS GIFFARD)

2 DASHES ANGOSTURA
BITTERS

3 OUNCES CHAMPAGNE

1½ OUNCES ICE-COLD
VANILLA BEAN VODKA

In a chilled small wine glass, combine the passion fruit liqueur and bitters, and top with the Champagne. Stir lightly to mix. Grab the vanilla vodka from the freezer and pour into a chilled shot glass. Serve them together, taking a sip of one and then the other, and enjoy accordingly.

VANILLA BEAN VODKA

MAKES 7 OUNCES

1 VANILLA BEAN POD, HALVED
LENGTHWISE

6 OUNCES VODKA,
PREFERABLY BELVEDERE

1 OUNCE GALLIANO
L'AUTENTICO LIQUEUR

Combine the vanilla bean pod and vodka in a small bottle or mason jar and infuse for at least 1 day, or to your taste. When you think the infusion has extracted enough of the vanilla flavor, strain it into a clean container. Add the Galliano, stir, then funnel the vodka back into the bottle for use. The vodka will keep, tightly sealed, indefinitely at room temperature. Freeze for 8 to 12 hours before consumption for optimal texture.

FINE À L'EAU

BY **REMY SAVAGE**

BAR NOUVEAU (PARIS)

Everything Remy Savage touches turns to (liquid) gold. As one of the world's leading voices on vacuum distillation in bars, he typically produces high-concept cocktails unattainable to the home bartender. But he also appreciates the nuances of a simple serve, crafted with exceptional ingredients. Take the Fine à l'Eau, a straightforward tiny Cognac highball served at Bar Nouveau, a cocktail that, Savage says, is "probably my favorite drink of all time."

It has historical significance, as it's a modern version of the classic French Cognac highball. And once batched together, the cocktail has a shelf life of up to a year. It's an expression of simplicity and provenance, and sometimes those characteristics make the best cocktails.

¾ OUNCE COGNAC	Chill the Cognac in the freezer, and the rest of the ingredients in the refrigerator, for at least 1 hour beforehand. Combine the Cognac, verjus, and Simple Syrup in a chilled lowball or tiny wine glass. Add the soda water and enjoy.
½ OUNCE VERJUS	
½ OUNCE SIMPLE SYRUP (PAGE 22)	
1 OUNCE SODA WATER	

HALF CENTURY

 This is a tiny rendition of the classic 20th Century cocktail, which is one of those gin cocktails that has flown under the radar since its creation by the British bartender C. A. Tuck in the early 1900s. At first glance, cacao and lemon may raise an eyebrow or two, but trust that this time-tested formula delivers an elegantly refreshing balance of sweet and sour, which sings in a chilled tiny cocktail glass.

¾ OUNCE GIN

2 TEASPOONS FRESHLY SQUEEZED LEMON JUICE

¼ OUNCE CREME DE CACAO

¼ OUNCE LILLET BLANC

Garnish: 1 LEMON TWIST

Combine the gin, lemon juice, creme de cacao, and Lillet Blanc in a shaker filled with ice and shake vigorously to chill and dilute. Strain into a chilled tiny coupe and garnish with the lemon twist.

LUMIA

BY **EZRA STAR**

MOSTLY HARMLESS BAR
(HONG KONG)

For her tiny cocktail Lumia, Ezra Star was inspired by memories of picking Lumia lemons in her current home city of Hong Kong after a typhoon. Star aimed to make a fragrant and fresh martini variation for her bar, Mostly Harmless, that really highlighted the perfumed notes of the lemons. This unorthodox tiny martini-meets-gimlet, stirred with fresh lemon juice and a lemon cordial, is precisely that.

½ OUNCE GIN

½ OUNCE LEMON CORDIAL

¼ OUNCE LEMON JUICE

¼ OUNCE DRY VERMOUTH

Garnish: 1 GRAPEFRUIT TWIST

Combine the gin, Lemon Cordial, lemon juice, and vermouth in a mixing glass filled with ice and stir to chill and dilute. Strain into a chilled tiny coupe or martini glass, and garnish with the grapefruit twist.

LEMON CORDIAL

MAKES ABOUT ⅓ CUP

PEELS OF 2 LEMONS, PREFERABLY LUMIA LEMONS

½ CUP SUGAR

¼ CUP JUST-BOILED WATER

In a container or zip seal bag, combine the lemon peels and sugar. Gently muddle to release some of the oils from the peels, and let the mixture rest for at least 1 hour, or overnight for maximum flavor. After the sugar has extracted the oils from the peels, creating an oleo saccharum, add the hot water to the mix to fully dissolve any remaining sugar. Let the cordial cool and come to room temp, and strain out the peels. Transfer to a bottle and store in the refrigerator, tightly sealed, for up to 1 month.

✳ BUILD A FLIGHT

Try a flight of Shakeratos using a different aperitivo for each one, such as Campari, Select Aperitivo, and one from a small craft producer, for example, St. George Spirits' Bruto Americano.

SHAKERATO

Need to whip up a cocktail in no time with the bare minimum? The Shakerato is the answer—that is, if you and your guests happen to be Negroni converts who enjoy bittersweet flavors. It's a customizable one-bottle cocktail: Pick any bottle of red aperitif—Campari or Select Aperitivo are a couple mainstream options, but craft producers are also producing some exceptional aperitifs. Shake it to hell with ice, as well as a dash of saline to tame the bitterness. The result is a refreshingly simple aperitif made on the fly. Dress it up with an expressed citrus peel and indulge in this abrasively bitter tipple, which will get the appetite stimulated in no time.

1¾ OUNCES APERITIVO BITTER (SUCH AS CAMPARI OR SELECT APERITIVO)

DASH OF SALINE SOLUTION OR PINCH OF SALT

Garnish: 1 ORANGE TWIST OR 1 LEMON TWIST OR BOTH

Combine the aperitivo bitter and Saline Solution in a shaker with ice and shake vigorously to chill and dilute. Strain into a chilled tiny coupe or martini glass. Garnish with the lemon or orange twist and serve.

→ SALINE SOLUTION

MAKES ⅓ CUP

⅓ CUP WARM WATER

4 TEASPOONS FINE SEA SALT

In a small bowl, combine the water and salt, and stir until the salt has dissolved. With a pipette, transfer to a small tincture bottle. Store, tightly sealed, in the refrigerator for up to 1 month.

NOTE: Most cocktails benefit from a dash of saline, so try it in any tiny cocktail in this book.

✳ BUILD A FLIGHT

Try the Spring Garden next to two
variations: one made with Acid-
Adjusted Grapefruit Juice (page
62) instead of the lemon juice, and
another made with Honey Syrup (page
23) instead of the Lavender-Honey
Syrup, for a classic Bee's Knees.

SPRING GARDEN

 Fresh, *floral*, and *familiar* sum up this approachable twist on the classic Bee's Knees. My take substitutes gin for genever, the national spirit of the Netherlands, which falls somewhere on the spectrum between gin and whiskey.

While a typical gin is bright, and heavy on the aromatic botanicals, genever is more reserved and subtle in flavor. It still expresses a high note of pine and lemon zest because of the juniper, a hallmark of genever. But it's grounded in a richer malt spirit, which marries beautifully with the Lavender-Honey Syrup in this cocktail.

---

1 OUNCE GENEVER
(SUCH AS BOLS)

HEAVY ¼ OUNCE
LEMON JUICE

HEAVY ¼ OUNCE LAVENDER-
HONEY SYRUP

Combine the genever, lemon juice, and Lavender-Honey Syrup in a shaker filled with ice and shake vigorously to chill and dilute. Strain into a chilled tiny coupe and enjoy the drink.

LAVENDER-HONEY SYRUP

MAKES ABOUT 1½ CUPS

½ CUP WATER

1 SMALL BUNCH DRIED
LAVENDER (7 GRAMS)

1 CUP HONEY

Combine the water and lavender in a saucepan and heat on medium-low for 5 minutes, bringing the water to a simmer to create a lavender tisane. Remove from the heat, slowly pour the honey into the saucepan, and stir to dissolve, 1 to 2 minutes. Let the syrup cool to room temperature. Strain the syrup through a fine-mesh strainer lined with cheesecloth and transfer to a bottle. Store in the refrigerator, tightly sealed, for up to 1 month.

SNAQUIRI

In 2010, bartender Karin Stanley of New York City's Dutch Kills was sitting at a bar with bartending legend Giuseppe Gonzalez when the Snaquiri was born. Over time, the Snaquiri has evolved into a small-format version of the beloved daiquiri, one of my favorite cocktails, most commonly consumed as a pre-shift drink by bartenders, or served to VIP guests as a hospitable way of saying hello or goodbye. It could be argued that this is the tiny cocktail that ushered in the era of small-format drinking, so its inclusion in this book is a given.

1 OUNCE LIGHTLY AGED WHITE RUM (SUCH AS DIPLOMATICO PLANAS)

½ OUNCE LIME JUICE

¼ OUNCE RICH SIMPLE SYRUP (SEE NOTE, PAGE 22)

Combine the rum, lime juice, and Rich Simple Syrup in a cocktail shaker with ice, and shake the mix until chilled and diluted. Double strain the cocktail into a tiny coupe or martini glass and enjoy.

NOTE: For a strawberry-flavored variation when the berries are in season, substitute Macerated Strawberry Syrup (page 115) for the Rich Simple Syrup.

NUCLEAR SNAQUIRI

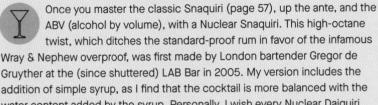 Once you master the classic Snaquiri (page 57), up the ante, and the ABV (alcohol by volume), with a Nuclear Snaquiri. This high-octane twist, which ditches the standard-proof rum in favor of the infamous Wray & Nephew overproof, was first made by London bartender Gregor de Gruyther at the (since shuttered) LAB Bar in 2005. My version includes the addition of simple syrup, as I find that the cocktail is more balanced with the water content added by the syrup. Personally, I wish every Nuclear Daiquiri was served in a tiny format. After trying this cocktail for yourself, I'm sure you'll understand why.

1 OUNCE JAMAICAN
OVERPROOF WHITE RUM
(SUCH AS WRAY & NEPHEW)

½ OUNCE GREEN
CHARTREUSE

½ OUNCE LIME JUICE

¼ OUNCE SIMPLE SYRUP
(PAGE 22)

Combine the rum, chartreuse, lime juice, and Simple Syrup in a cocktail shaker with ice, and shake the mix until it's chilled and diluted. Then strain the cocktail into a tiny coupe or martini glass and enjoy.

NOTE: The Acid-Adjusted Grapefruit Juice is the key to a balanced and surprising take on the margarita, but you can substitute ¼ ounce freshly squeezed lime juice plus ¼ ounce freshly squeezed grapefruit juice. (Be sure to include the lime juice. The grapefruit juice is not acidic enough on its own to balance the sweetness.)

FIESTA ON WARREN

This cocktail is a scaled-down version of the first drink I created for the opening menu at Lawrence Park, in Hudson, New York. Named after the bar's street address, this grapefruit-laced twist on the mezcal margarita was designed to be a crowd-pleasing party starter (per the name). Unsurprisingly—who doesn't love a good marg?—it was one of the bar's best-selling drinks when it opened in 2019, and it's a serve that I still make at home from time to time when I fancy a nostalgic taste from one of my favorite places to drink in the world.

SALT FOR RIMMING
THE GLASS

½ OUNCE ACID-ADJUSTED
GRAPEFRUIT JUICE
(PAGE 62)

½ OUNCE BLANCO TEQUILA

¼ OUNCE BLANC VERMOUTH,
PREFERABLY LA QUINTINYE

½ OUNCE MEZCAL,
PREFERABLY DERRUMBES
SAN LUIS POTOSÍ

¼ OUNCE AGAVE SYRUP
(PAGE 23)

DASH OF SALINE
SOLUTION (PAGE 53)
OR PINCH OF SALT

Garnish: ¼ OR ½ GRAPEFRUIT
WHEEL (DEPENDING ON SIZE)

If you wish, rim a chilled tiny rocks glass with salt. Put a couple of small chunks of clear ice into the glass. Combine the Acid-Adjusted Grapefruit Juice, tequila, vermouth, mezcal, Agave Syrup, and Saline Solution in a shaker filled with ice, shake vigorously to chill and dilute, and strain over the ice in the rocks glass. Garnish with the grapefruit wheel and enjoy.

CONTINUES

ACID-ADJUSTED GRAPEFRUIT JUICE

MAKES ABOUT 1 CUP

8½ OUNCES FRESHLY
SQUEEZED GRAPEFRUIT JUICE

HEAPING 1¼ TEASPOONS
CITRIC ACID POWDER

1 TEASPOON MALIC ACID
POWDER

In a container, combine the grapefruit juice and acid powders and stir until the powders are dissolved. Transfer to a bottle and store, tightly sealed, in the refrigerator and use within 1 week for optimal freshness.

> **NOTE:** For a simple twist, substitute Acid-Adjusted Grapefruit Juice for lime juice or lemon juice, for example, in the Nuclear Snaquiri (page 59) or the Spring Garden (page 55).

TAKING THE BULL BY THE HORNS

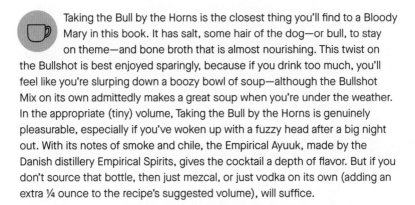

Taking the Bull by the Horns is the closest thing you'll find to a Bloody Mary in this book. It has salt, some hair of the dog—or bull, to stay on theme—and bone broth that is almost nourishing. This twist on the Bullshot is best enjoyed sparingly, because if you drink too much, you'll feel like you're slurping down a boozy bowl of soup—although the Bullshot Mix on its own admittedly makes a great soup when you're under the weather. In the appropriate (tiny) volume, Taking the Bull by the Horns is genuinely pleasurable, especially if you've woken up with a fuzzy head after a big night out. With its notes of smoke and chile, the Empirical Ayuuk, made by the Danish distillery Empirical Spirits, gives the cocktail a depth of flavor. But if you don't source that bottle, then just mezcal, or just vodka on its own (adding an extra ¼ ounce to the recipe's suggested volume), will suffice.

2 OUNCES BULLSHOT MIX (PAGE 65)	Heat the Bullshot Mix in the microwave or on the stovetop over medium heat until simmering. Pour the mix into a ceramic cup, add the vodka and Ayuuk, and enjoy.
½ OUNCE VODKA	
¼ OUNCE EMPIRICAL AYUUK OR MEZCAL	

CONTINUES

BULLSHOT MIX

MAKES ABOUT 1½ CUPS

½ CUP BEEF BONE BROTH
(SUCH AS BONAFIDE
PROVISIONS ORGANIC) OR
CONSOMMÉ, AT ROOM
TEMPERATURE

½ OUNCE OLOROSO SHERRY

¼ OUNCE LEMON JUICE

¼ OUNCE SOY SAUCE

¾ TEASPOON
WORCESTERSHIRE SAUCE

¼ TEASPOON FRESHLY GROUND
BLACK PEPPER

Combine bone broth, sherry, lemon juice, soy
sauce, Worcestershire sauce, and pepper in a
bowl and stir to combine. Pour into an airtight
bottle or container and store, tightly sealed, in
the refrigerator for up to 1 week.

GOLDEN

BY **AGOSTINO PERRONE**

THE CONNAUGHT BAR
(LONDON)

I'll never forget my first experience at London's award-winning Connaught Bar, named for the historic hotel in which it sits. It was November 2019—my first time in London, visiting the woman who I now have the privilege of calling my wife. I was jet-lagged and semi-delirious—and the photos I have show as much—but the excitement of new love and drinking at one of my bucket-list hotel bars stifled those relatively insignificant states of being.

For my fellow cocktail lovers who've never had the luxury of drinking at the Connaught Bar, it exudes a timeless magic and sophistication that few other bars are able to match. And the guy at the helm, who has shaped the bar into the legendary destination that it's become since helping it open in 2008, is the inimitable Agostino Perrone. On arrival, each guest at the Connaught Bar is offered a miniature amuse-bouche, which varies with the season and occasion. Golden is one of these special welcome drinks. Now, thanks to Ago, you can enjoy a taste of the legendary Connaught Bar at home.

¾ OUNCE BLANCO TEQUILA

¾ OUNCE GRAPEFRUIT SHERBET (PAGE 68)

¾ OUNCE BREWED JASMINE TEA, COOLED TO ROOM TEMPERATURE

1 TEASPOON GALLIANO L'AUTENTICO

Combine the tequila, Grapefruit Sherbet, jasmine tea, and Galliano in a cocktail shaker with ice and shake to chill and dilute. Strain into a chilled tiny coupe and serve.

CONTINUES

GRAPEFRUIT SHERBET

MAKES ABOUT ⅔ CUP

PEELS FROM 1 MEDIUM GRAPEFRUIT

¼ CUP SUPERFINE SUGAR

½ CUP FRESH GRAPEFRUIT JUICE

Combine the grapefruit peel and sugar in a bowl and lightly muddle to extract the oils from the peel. Let the mixture rest for at least 30 minutes, and ideally 2 to 4 hours, so the sugar can extract most of the oils from the peels. Pour in the grapefruit juice, and stir until the sugar is dissolved completely. Strain the sherbet through a fine-mesh strainer into a bottle. Store, tightly sealed, in the refrigerator until needed for 4 to 7 days.

DEVITO

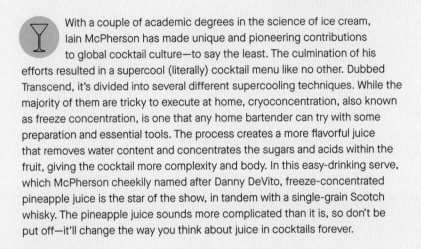

BY **IAIN MCPHERSON**

PANDA & SONS, HOOT THE REDEEMER, AND NAUTICUS (EDINBURGH)

B A R T E N D E R R E C I P E

With a couple of academic degrees in the science of ice cream, Iain McPherson has made unique and pioneering contributions to global cocktail culture—to say the least. The culmination of his efforts resulted in a supercool (literally) cocktail menu like no other. Dubbed Transcend, it's divided into several different supercooling techniques. While the majority of them are tricky to execute at home, cryoconcentration, also known as freeze concentration, is one that any home bartender can try with some preparation and essential tools. The process creates a more flavorful juice that removes water content and concentrates the sugars and acids within the fruit, giving the cocktail more complexity and body. In this easy-drinking serve, which McPherson cheekily named after Danny DeVito, freeze-concentrated pineapple juice is the star of the show, in tandem with a single-grain Scotch whisky. The pineapple juice sounds more complicated than it is, so don't be put off—it'll change the way you think about juice in cocktails forever.

---

1 OUNCE SINGLE-GRAIN SCOTCH, SUCH AS HAIG CLUB CLUBMAN

½ OUNCE BIANCO VERMOUTH

½ OUNCE FREEZE-CONCENTRATED PINEAPPLE JUICE (PAGE 71)

DASH OF ANGOSTURA BITTERS

Garnish: 1 SMALL PINEAPPLE WEDGE

Combine the scotch, vermouth, Freeze-Concentrated Pineapple Juice, and bitters in a cocktail shaker with ice and shake vigorously. Double strain into a tiny coupe or martini glass, garnish with the pineapple wedge, and enjoy.

CONTINUES

FREEZE-CONCENTRATED PINEAPPLE JUICE

MAKES ABOUT 1¼ CUP

2 CUPS PINEAPPLE JUICE

Pour the pineapple juice into an insulated container and put it in the freezer until the top layer is well frozen, 6 to 12 hours. Remove the frozen layer of ice by pouring the juice through a strainer (the frozen layer on top may have to be gently broken apart before straining). The remaining liquid is the freeze-concentrated pineapple juice. Transfer it to a bottle and store, tightly sealed, in the refrigerator for up to 2 weeks.

NOTE: Swap this infused mezcal for the standard mezcal in Fiesta on Warren (page 61).

NAKED & INFAMOUS

This twist on New York City bartender Joaquín Simó's Naked & Famous stays true to the classic formula, with just two main adjustments. The first is Hibiscus-Infused Mezcal instead of standard mezcal, and the second is Bénédictine to replace the yellow Chartreuse. The latter is, for all intents and purposes, a like-for-like swap—I just dial back the volume as Bénédictine is a touch sweeter than yellow Chartreuse. The infused mezcal adds tannins to the cocktail, which helps maintain its structure and balance, and it deepens the drink's reddish-pink hue, adding to its visual appeal. For agave spirit lovers, this is one hell of a welcome drink, and a relatively straightforward one to whip up, at that.

½ OUNCE APEROL

½ OUNCE LIME JUICE

¼ OUNCE BÉNÉDICTINE

½ OUNCE HIBISCUS-INFUSED MEZCAL

Garnish: 1 LIME TWIST

Combine the Aperol, lime juice, Bénédictine, and Hibiscus-Infused Mezcal in a cocktail shaker with ice and shake vigorously. Strain into a chilled tiny coupe and garnish with the lime twist.

→ HIBISCUS-INFUSED MEZCAL

MAKES 6 OUNCES

2 TABLESPOONS OR 2 GRAMS OF DRIED HIBISCUS FLOWERS

6 OUNCES MEZCAL

Combine the mezcal and hibiscus flowers in a jar or container and let it sit for 1 hour at room temperature. Strain through a fine-mesh strainer lined with cheesecloth to remove the solids and transfer to a clean bottle. Store, tightly sealed, at room temperature, or in the refrigerator, for up to 3 months.

ANOMALY

 The Anomaly, as the name hints at, is one of those cocktails that deviates from classic cocktail structure. It has traces of both the martini and the sour in its balance of ingredients. Like the martini, it's unmistakably boozy and light, but it has the freshness and balanced sweetness of a succulent sour. Anomaly matches neither template identically though. Instead, this sophisticated drink strikes a harmonious balance of fortifying spirit with sugar and acid, allowing the seamless pairing of smoky mezcal and tropical banana to take center stage. In a way, it's a gateway cocktail to more spirituous cocktails. It's easy to throw back, but do tread lightly: A few of these tiny yet bold libations and your legs might just turn into noodles.

¾ OUNCE MEZCAL

¼ OUNCE FINO SHERRY

¼ OUNCE BANANA LIQUEUR,
PREFERABLY TEMPUS FUGIT

⅓ OUNCE (2 TEASPOONS)
VERJUS

1 BARSPOON SIMPLE SYRUP
(PAGE 22) OR AGAVE SYRUP
(PAGE 23)

Garnish: 1 TINY LEMON PEEL
COIN (SEE NOTE)

Combine the mezcal, sherry, banana liqueur, verjus, and Simple Syrup in a mixing glass with ice. Stir to chill and dilute, and strain into a chilled tiny coupe. Garnish with the lemon peel coin.

NOTE: Use a clean, medium-sized hole puncher to make this garnish.

MISO GOLD RUSH

The classic Gold Rush (bourbon, honey syrup, and lemon juice) is one of the most influential cocktails of the modern era. Created by T. J. Siegal at the pioneering Milk & Honey, in New York City, in 2001, the drink became a modern classic, recognized and served in bars all around the world. It was also the base recipe for bartender Sam Ross's iconic Penicillin cocktail.

My Miso Gold Rush is a subtle twist on Siegal's perfected recipe. Instead of the standard honey syrup, I use a richer Miso-Honey Syrup, which adds a sweet-umami flavor to the drink, which goes hand in hand with bourbon. It's the perfect, invigorating whiskey cocktail to serve during the winter as a welcome drink, or for the whiskey doubters who haven't been sold on the spirit—yet. A taste of the Miso Gold Rush may just lure them to the dark side (of spirits, of course).

---

1 OUNCE BOURBON

⅓ OUNCE MISO-HONEY SYRUP

2 TEASPOONS LEMON JUICE

Garnish: 1 PIECE OF HONEYCOMB (OPTIONAL)

Put a tiny chunk of clear ice in a chilled tiny rocks glass. If you like, lay a piece of honeycomb on the ice. Combine the bourbon, Miso-Honey Syrup, and lemon juice in a cocktail shaker with ice and shake to chill and dilute. Strain the drink into the rocks glass and serve.

MISO-HONEY SYRUP

MAKES ABOUT ½ CUP

½ CUP HONEY SYRUP (PAGE 23)

1 TABLESPOON WHITE MISO

With a hand blender, blend the Honey Syrup and miso in a deep bowl or container. Strain through a fine-mesh strainer and transfer to a bottle. Store in the refrigerator, tightly sealed, for up to 1 month.

NOTE: This syrup is best made when ingredients are weighed. To weigh, first weigh the Honey Syrup. The white miso should be 15 percent of the weight of the syrup.

TINY NEGRONI

As famous as it's become, and as delicious as it is to seasoned Negroni drinkers, this Italian classic remains an acquired taste. The bittersweet mixture of gin, sweet vermouth, and Campari is an initial smack in the face—it's floral, botanical-forward, and undoubtedly spirituous. But once that powerful shock to the system subsides, what's left is a balanced, bright-red aperitivo cocktail that promptly stimulates the appetite and begs to be paired with some cicchetti (small snacks). The classic calls for an equal part of each ingredient, but I prefer a Negroni that allows the base spirit to shine, so I up the gin a touch and recommend that you do the same.

¾ OUNCE GIN

½ OUNCE SWEET VERMOUTH

½ OUNCE CAMPARI

Garnish: 1 ORANGE PEEL

Stir the gin, vermouth, and Campari in a mixing glass with ice to full dilution (since it's being served up instead of over ice, the mix will need to be stirred for 30 to 35 revolutions). Strain the contents into a chilled tiny coupe. Express the orange peel over the cocktail and then discard.

✳ BUILD A FLIGHT

There are many different takes on the classic Negroni, but here are two that are definitely worth your while. For a Oaxacan Negroni, substitute ¾ ounce mezcal for the gin. And for a Boulevardier, substitute ¾ ounce bourbon for the gin. Taste all three to see how they vary while staying true to the original.

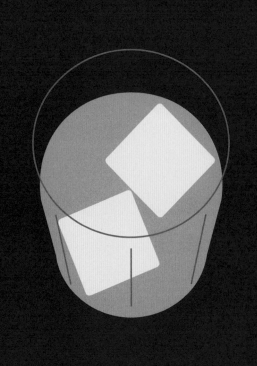

NIGHTCAPS

To punctuate the end of a convivial, cocktail-filled evening, it's common practice to enjoy a nightcap. The term was coined in the nineteenth century during a time when cloth nightcaps—cozy caps worn at night to keep one's head warm while sleeping—were in vogue. But in modern times, when the headwear (thankfully) fell out of fashion, the "nightcap" has become synonymous with the final drink of an evening.

As Kara Newman, the author of *Nightcap* (2018), makes clear: "It's not just a singular type of drink." In fact, the nightcaps we drink are as personal as the music we listen to, cultures we subscribe to, and beliefs we garner through our unique lived experiences. Although this is what makes them difficult to define, they are all the more enjoyable as a result.

In the cocktail bar industry, it's common for a bartender to serve a friend or colleague an unsolicited tiny nightcap as a hospitable way to say, "Goodnight, and thanks for stopping by." It's a little liquid manifestation of a hug goodbye, and it translates seamlessly into the context of home drinking (especially if you want to leave guests with a positive impression of the evening).

Whether you are seeking a cocktail to continue the conversation with a friend at the end of an evening, to fulfill the role of dessert, to help aid digestion, or to simply leave your palate filled with a flavor that you can enjoy until you brush your teeth before bed, this chapter of tiny nightcaps has you sorted.

NIGHTS IN JALISCO

Mezcal didn't really become popular in cocktail culture until the mid-
to late aughts, picking up steam in Boston, thanks to the likes of the
"godmother of mezcal," Misty Kalkofen, and New York City, thanks to
bartender Phil Ward. Since then, cocktails such as the Oaxacan Old-Fashioned
and the Naked and Famous have firmly established themselves in mainstream
cocktail culture globally. Had Nights in Jalisco debuted back then at one of
these influential cocktail bars, I like to think that today it would be a modern
classic. It's big and bold in flavor, with notes of smoke, chocolate, mint, raisin,
and sweet roasted agave, so it's a cocktail that goes the distance in tiny form.
Give it a taste and you'll see what I'm talking about.

¾ OUNCE AÑEJO TEQUILA	Combine the tequila, mezcal, sherry, and amaro in a mixing glass filled with ice and stir to chill and dilute. Strain into a tiny coupe and garnish with the olive.
¼ OUNCE MEZCAL	
¼ OUNCE PX (PEDRO XIMÉNEZ) SHERRY	
1 HEAPING BARSPOON OF BRAULIO AMARO	
Garnish: 1 KALAMATA OLIVE, CHILLED	

THE CAMBRIDGE

In 2014, while a college student in Cambridge, Massachusetts, I was drinking with my best friend at a bar and restaurant called Alden & Harlow. There was a sour-style cocktail on the menu that listed mushroom as one of the ingredients. While I was put off by the peculiar addition, my more adventurous friend decided to go for it. And I'll forever be grateful that he did, because it was that cocktail that changed the way I think about flavor in drinks and set me on my path in the drinks industry.

The Cambridge is an homage to that experience. This complex elixir sits somewhere between an old-fashioned and a Manhattan, and is utterly delicious. I use bourbon as the base, but this also works exceptionally well with Cognac or an aged rum. And if you can find some truffle honey, using that in the honey syrup will really take this to the next level.

1 OUNCE BOURBON

½ OUNCE SWEET VERMOUTH, PREFERABLY COCCHI DI TORINO

1 BARSPOON AMONTILLADO SHERRY

1 BARSPOON TRUFFLE HONEY SYRUP (SEE NOTE)

DASH OF BITTERMENS MOLE BITTERS

Garnish: 1 ORANGE PEEL

Put a chunk of clear ice into a tiny rocks glass. Add the bourbon, vermouth, sherry, Truffle Honey Syrup, and bitters to a mixing glass and briefly stir with ice until chilled, and strain over the ice in the rocks glass. Express the orange peel over the cocktail and then discard.

NOTE: To make the Truffle Honey Syrup, follow the directions for Honey Syrup on page 23, substituting truffle honey for the regular honey.

THE DIPLOMAT

In his 1862 book *How to Mix Drinks*, cocktail pioneer Jerry Thomas shared the recipe for his nutty and sweet Japanese Cocktail. The cocktail, which has no trace of Japanese flavors, is believed to have been inspired by a member of Japan's first diplomatic mission to the United States, Tateishi Onojirou-Noriyuki, who spent many nights drinking in Thomas's saloon on Broadway. The classic version is a simple stirred cocktail made with Cognac, orgeat, and Angostura bitters. To create the Diplomat, I refined the recipe by including a touch of vermouth and bittersweet Cynar for depth of flavor and balance.

1 OUNCE RYE WHISKEY, PREFERABLY 100-PROOF

¼ OUNCE SUNFLOWER SEED AND ALMOND ORGEAT (PAGE 88)

¼ OUNCE DRY VERMOUTH (SUCH AS BALDORIA UMAMI)

1 TEASPOON CYNAR

Garnish: 1 LEMON TWIST

Combine the whiskey, Sunflower Seed and Almond Orgeat, vermouth, and Cynar in a mixing glass with ice and stir to chill and dilute. Strain into a chilled tiny coupe and garnish with the lemon twist.

CONTINUES

SUNFLOWER SEED AND ALMOND ORGEAT

MAKES ABOUT 2 CUPS

1 CUP SLICED ALMONDS

½ CUP SUNFLOWER SEEDS

1½ CUPS WATER

2¼ CUPS SUGAR

½ TEASPOON ORANGE
BLOSSOM WATER

½ TEASPOON VODKA

Heat a dry medium skillet over low-medium heat and toast the almonds and sunflower seeds until pale gold and fragrant, stirring constantly, about 3 to 4 minutes. Put the toasted nuts and seeds in a food processor or blender and lightly pulse for 10 to 15 seconds. Transfer to a large container, add the water, and let it sit, tightly covered, in the refrigerator, for at least 8 hours. Strain the mixture through a strainer lined with cheesecloth, or through a nut milk bag, into another large container, squeezing the cheesecloth or bag to get out all the liquid. Finally, add the sugar, orange blossom water, and vodka and stir until the sugar is completely dissolved. If the sugar doesn't dissolve, transfer the mixture to a saucepan and heat over low heat, stirring to dissolve the sugar. Cool to room temperature. Transfer the orgeat to a bottle and store, tightly sealed, in the refrigerator for up to 1 month.

HG WALTER OLD-FASHIONED

 Inspired by Don Lee's famous Benton's Old-Fashioned, the PDT-born-and-bred drink that paved the way for all the other fat-washed cocktails (see page 21), the HG Walter Old-Fashioned is my British take on the American classic.

Similar to Lee's serve, named after the producer that he sourced his bacon from, I've named this savory old-fashioned after the popular English bacon producer and butcher H. G. Walter. Instead of using a bacon fat–washed bourbon base, I opt for an aged rum instead, because of its growing popularity in the UK and its subtle sweetness, which pairs well with the salty fat of the bacon. It's an indulgent flavor bomb of a tiny cocktail, and it lends itself well to being enjoyed in small doses.

1 OUNCE BACON FAT–WASHED AGED RUM (PAGE 91)

¼ OUNCE PEATED SCOTCH, PREFERABLY BOWMORE 12 YEAR

1 BARSPOON GRADE-A MAPLE SYRUP

1 DASH BITTERMENS XOCOLATL MOLE BITTERS

Garnish: 1 ORANGE PEEL COIN

Put a chunk of clear ice in a chilled tiny rocks glass. Combine the Bacon Fat–Washed Aged Rum, scotch, maple syrup, and bitters in a mixing glass filled with ice and stir to chill (see Note). Strain the cocktail over the ice in the rocks glass and flame the orange coin (see page 91). Place the coin on the ice and enjoy.

NOTE: Do not stir the drink to full dilution as you would a Manhattan or martini, because when the ice in the glass begins to melt, the cocktail will be overdiluted.

CONTINUES

BACON FAT-WASHED AGED RUM

MAKES ABOUT 8 OUNCES

4 STRIPS BACON

8 OUNCES AGED RUM

Cook the bacon in a skillet over medium heat until done to your liking. Strain the bacon fat through a fine-mesh strainer. Transfer the fat, approximately ¾ ounce, into a container or mason jar and discard the rest. Stir in the rum. Set aside the mixture for 4 hours to infuse, reheating briefly in the microwave if the fat starts to solidify. (Alternatively, if you have an immersion circulator, cook sous vide at 120°F for the same length of time.) Place the container in the freezer until the fat has solidified, at least 2 hours, or overnight. Remove the container from the freezer and strain the infused rum through a fine-mesh strainer lined with cheesecloth. Transfer the infused rum to a bottle and store, tightly sealed, in the refrigerator for up to 2 weeks.

> **NOTE:** Because this fat wash calls for animal fat, refrigeration is crucial to ensure the infusion is safe for consumption.

HOW TO FLAME AN ORANGE PEEL COIN

To flame an orange peel coin, light a match and hold it over the drink. With your other hand, hold the orange coin above the flame, and express the oils of the orange peel through it. The oils will caramelize, creating a softer and sweeter orange note, which lends itself well to spirit-forward cocktails made with aged spirits, such as whiskey, rum, and brandy.

A PROPER MARTINEZ

The Martinez, the martini's progenitor, is often cited as a cocktail made with gin. And while that's true, according to O. H. Byron's 1884 *The Modern Bartenders' Guide*, which first printed the Martinez recipe as we know it, it's likely that the "gin" was the Dutch genever, the more popular style of juniper-infused spirit in the United States at the time. I had never had a Martinez made with genever until my first visit to the Netherlands in 2018. It was like all the stars aligned, and I saw the light for the first time. *This is the way a Martinez should taste*, I thought to myself. So, now it's time for you to decide: Does this taste like a proper Martinez? The cocktail is fit for elongating an evening filled with riveting conversation, so try both versions—with gin and with genever—to find out.

¾ OUNCE GENEVER (SUCH AS BOLS)

¾ OUNCE SWEET VERMOUTH (SUCH AS CARPANO ANTICA)

1 TEASPOON MARASCHINO LIQUEUR (SUCH AS LUXARDO)

DASH OF ANGOSTURA BITTERS

Garnish: 1 ORANGE PEEL

Combine the genever, vermouth, maraschino liqueur, and bitters in a mixing glass with ice and stir to chill and dilute. Strain into a chilled tiny martini glass, express the orange peel over the drink, discard, and enjoy the cocktail.

✳ BUILD A FLIGHT

Accompany the Proper Martinez with a second Martinez made with Chamomile-Infused Gin (page 121), and a third one made with equal parts London dry gin and genever.

BAR HOPPER

Sometimes the best dessert comes in liquid form, and this cocktail is the perfect manifestation of that notion. The Bar Hopper is my twist on the decadent grasshopper, the ultimate nightcap, which is traditionally concocted with equal parts crème de cacao, crème de menthe, and heavy cream. In a total commitment to the liquid dessert vibe, I finish the Bar Hopper with a generous flurry of chocolate shavings. It's a cocktail that I personally prefer in smaller volumes because of its richness. Bar Hopper is best crafted with premium ingredients because of the cocktail's relative simplicity.

½ OUNCE FERNET BRANCA

¼ OUNCE CRÈME DE CACAO, PREFERABLY TEMPUS FUGIT

1 TEASPOON CRÈME DE MENTHE, PREFERABLY TEMPUS FUGIT

1 TEASPOON COGNAC

½ OUNCE HEAVY CREAM

Garnish: CHUNK OF BITTERSWEET CHOCOLATE FOR SHAVING

Combine the Fernet Branca, crème de cacao, crème de menthe, Cognac, and heavy cream in a cocktail shaker with ice and shake vigorously to chill and dilute. Strain the cocktail into a chilled tiny coupe and shave the chocolate directly onto the drink to garnish.

SEAFIRE COLADA

There are few cocktails that I think about as often as the Escape, an elegant twist on the Champagne piña colada, served at the Kimpton Seafire Resort & Spa in Grand Cayman. And it's not only because it's a drink that I shared with my wife when we first met but also because the tropical tipple is exceptionally delicious and easy to replicate.

Created by the hotel's beverage manager Jim Wrigley, the Escape is a refined balance of coconut- and pineapple-infused rums, accented with fresh lime and pineapple juices and Coco Lopez coconut cream, and topped with cava, which gives the drink a fluffy head. I remain true to the essence of Jim's Escape cocktail, but I simplify the recipe for swift execution at home. The indulgence of this drink, which feels like a mini meal, makes the Seafire Colada an ideal nightcap. It's one of my favorite cocktails, and lends itself well to a smaller format, given the richness of the creamy Coco Lopez. After a little taste of this liquid ray of sunshine, I think it might become a favorite of yours, too.

¾ OUNCE LIGHTLY AGED WHITE RUM (SUCH AS PROBITAS)

½ OUNCE COCO LOPEZ COCONUT CREAM

¼ OUNCE FRESH PINEAPPLE JUICE

¼ OUNCE LIME JUICE

SPLASH OF CHAMPAGNE

Combine the rum, coconut cream, and juices in a cocktail shaker filled with ice and briefly shake to chill. Strain into a tiny snifter glass and top with Champagne.

NOTE: To take this drink to the next level, freeze the batched Dodo Manhattan for 6 to 12 hours before serving and serve it ice-cold.

DODO MANHATTAN

BY **RYAN
CHETIYAWARDANA**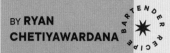

SUPER LYAN (AMSTERDAM),
LYANESS (LONDON), **SEED
LIBRARY** (LONDON), AND **SILVER
LYAN** (WASHINGTON, D.C.)

Ryan Chetiyawardana, also known as Mr. Lyan, is one of the most accomplished and influential bartenders of the modern era. His influence on contemporary cocktail technique, sustainability behind the bar, and overall innovation cannot be understated.

Over the course of his career, Chetiyawardana and his team have advocated for small-format drinks in an effort to keep flavors precise and showcase the best of a drink. And at home, Chetiyawardana enjoys tiny glassware to deliver the right "flavor punch," as he describes it. His low-ABV Manhattan-style serve is packed with complexity. For effortless service, Chetiyawardana recommends pre-batching a larger volume of the full cocktail and pouring individual serves so you can enjoy your guests' company while keeping them satiated. The Fruit-Infused Pineau des Charentes is also a lovely aperitif to enjoy on its own or served long with tonic water.

MAKES ABOUT 8 COCKTAILS

4 OUNCES FRUIT-INFUSED
PINEAU DES CHARENTES
(PAGE 100)

4 OUNCES SAUTERNES

6 OUNCES BOURBON

¾ OUNCE HEAVILY
PEATED SCOTCH (SUCH AS
LAPHROAIG)

¼ OUNCE PEYCHAUD'S
BITTERS

2 OUNCES WATER

Combine the Fruit-Infused Pineau des Charentes, Sauternes, bourbon, scotch, bitters, and water in a neutral container, stirring to blend. Transfer to a bottle and freeze for at least 1 hour before serving. To serve, pour 1½ to 2 ounces into a chilled mini tulip or tasting glass.

CONTINUES

FRUIT-INFUSED PINEAU DES CHARENTES

MAKES ABOUT 9 OUNCES

1 PASSION FRUIT, HALVED

1 SLICE FRESH GUAVA

1 BANANA, SLICED

8 OUNCES PINEAU DES CHARENTES

Scoop the passion fruit flesh into a sanitized bowl and add the guava, banana, and Pineau des Charentes. Stir gently to blend, cover, and refrigerate for 4 hours to let the wine become infused. Pour the wine through a strainer lined with cheesecloth or a coffee filter and transfer to a bottle. The wine will keep, tightly sealed, in the refrigerator for up to 1 month.

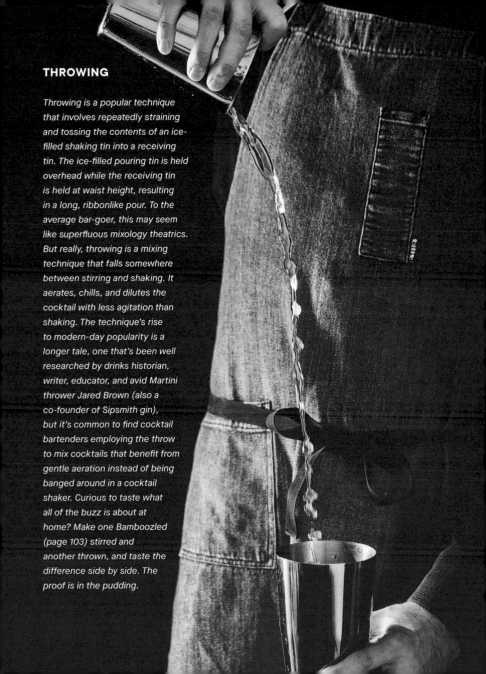

THROWING

Throwing is a popular technique that involves repeatedly straining and tossing the contents of an ice-filled shaking tin into a receiving tin. The ice-filled pouring tin is held overhead while the receiving tin is held at waist height, resulting in a long, ribbonlike pour. To the average bar-goer, this may seem like superfluous mixology theatrics. But really, throwing is a mixing technique that falls somewhere between stirring and shaking. It aerates, chills, and dilutes the cocktail with less agitation than shaking. The technique's rise to modern-day popularity is a longer tale, one that's been well researched by drinks historian, writer, educator, and avid Martini thrower Jared Brown (also a co-founder of Sipsmith gin), but it's common to find cocktail bartenders employing the throw to mix cocktails that benefit from gentle aeration instead of being banged around in a cocktail shaker. Curious to taste what all of the buzz is about at home? Make one Bamboozled (page 103) stirred and another thrown, and taste the difference side by side. The proof is in the pudding.

BAMBOOZLED

This twist on the classic Bamboo cocktail—traditionally a mix of dry sherry, vermouth, and bitters—is a reverse-engineered number inspired by a cocktail I had paired with a dessert at the end of a perfectly paced chef's table tasting menu. It was a refreshing alternative to the typical pour of some sweet wine.

The fresh, fortified, and aromatized wine base allows the drink to be seamlessly paired with food; the rum adds structure and a fine alcoholic backbone to the otherwise low-ABV tipple; and it's seasoned beautifully with notes of citrus. It's so simple, yet so delicious. It's the perfect accompaniment to an array of foods, and delightful in small doses.

½ OUNCE FINO SHERRY

½ OUNCE MARTINI RISERVA SPECIALE AMBRATO VERMOUTH OR BLANC VERMOUTH

1 OUNCE AGED RUM

¼ OUNCE GRAPEFRUIT LIQUEUR (SUCH AS GIFFARD PAMPLEMOUSSE)

DASH OF ORANGE BITTERS

Garnish: 1 ORANGE TWIST

Combine the sherry, vermouth, rum, grapefruit liqueur, and bitters in a mixing glass with ice and stir to chill and dilute. Strain into a tiny coupe, and garnish with the orange twist.

FRENCH KISS

A pairing that repeatedly appears in all sorts of sweets and desserts is chocolate and orange. It's simple and familiar, and most people have childhood memories of enjoying these two complementary flavors together, especially in Britain, where Terry's Chocolate Orange is a Christmastime staple. Using this popular flavor combination as the inspiration for this serve, I created a nuanced, two-part tiny nightcap that captures the essence of this flavor profile. It's the liquid equivalent of a sweet kiss goodnight, and the inclusion of a sweet, cacao-laced French brandy makes the playful name a no-brainer.

1 OUNCE CACAO NIB–INFUSED ARMAGNAC

    ½ OUNCE AMARO MONTENEGRO

    DASH OF SALINE SOLUTION (PAGE 53) OR PINCH OF SALT

    Garnish: 1 ORANGE PEEL

Combine the Cacao Nib–Infused Armagnac, amaro, and Saline Solution in a mixing glass filled with ice and stir to chill and dilute the cocktail. Strain into a chilled tiny coupe or tasting glass. Express the orange peel over the drink, discard, and serve.

→ CACAO NIB–INFUSED ARMAGNAC

MAKES 7 OUNCES

7 OUNCES ARMAGNAC

1½ TABLESPOONS RAW CACAO NIBS

Put the cacao nibs in a mason jar and pour the Armagnac over the cacao nibs. Set aside for 2 hours while the spirit becomes infused. Strain the infused Armagnac into a bottle and store, tightly sealed, in the refrigerator. Use within 1 month for best flavor.

BANANA BREAD

Among family and friends, my mom is known as the queen of banana bread. Powdered with cinnamon before it's baked and to finish, it evokes, without fail, feelings of nostalgia anytime I catch a whiff of it. Maybe this vivid food memory has shaped my insatiable desire for banana-flavored cocktails. In any case, it felt fitting to create a tiny cocktail dedicated to this significant food that always reminds me of my mother. Becherovka and banana in a spirituous, Sazerac-style cocktail can be a lot of flavor for the average palate, so serving this tipple as a taster is like a delicious little shot in the arm. You could also use absinthe to rinse the glass, but the Becherovka's notes of baking spices will really amplify the cinnamon in the syrup, so it's worth seeking out.

BECHEROVKA LIQUEUR OR ABSINTHE FOR RINSING

½ OUNCE SHERRY CASK AGED OR FINISHED SCOTCH (SUCH AS GLENDRONACH 12)

½ OUNCE RYE WHISKEY

1 TEASPOON BANANA LIQUEUR, PREFERABLY GIFFARD BANANE DU BRÉSIL

1 BARSPOON CINNAMON–EARL GREY SYRUP (PAGE 108)

DASH OF ANGOSTURA BITTERS

Garnish: 1 LEMON TWIST

Rinse the mixing glass with a dash of Becherovka and pour out the excess (or drink it). Fill the mixing glass with ice, add the scotch, whiskey, banana liqueur, Cinnamon–Earl Grey Syrup, and bitters, and stir to chill and dilute. Strain the cocktail into a chilled tiny rocks or martini glass and garnish with the lemon twist.

CONTINUES

CINNAMON–EARL GREY SYRUP

MAKES ABOUT 1½ CUPS

1 EARL GREY TEA BAG

1 CUP FRESHLY BOILED WATER

1 CUP GRANULATED SUGAR

2 CINNAMON STICKS

In a mug or measuring cup, steep the tea bag in the boiled water for 10 to 20 minutes. Meanwhile, put the sugar and cinnamon sticks in a heatproof bowl.

Remove the tea bag and reboil the tea. Pour the tea over the sugar and cinnamon sticks, and stir the syrup to help the sugar completely dissolve. Cover and let the cinnamon infuse the syrup for 2 to 4 hours (the longer the better). Strain the syrup into a bottle and store, tightly sealed, in the refrigerator for up to 1 month.

NOTE: Try this syrup in the Spring Garden (page 55) in place of the Lavender-Honey Syrup.

DUKE OF SUFFOLK

BY **GIUSEPPE GONZALEZ**

MOTT 32 (LAS VEGAS)

Utter the name Giuseppe Gonzalez to any proper bartender and he'll know who you're talking about. Gonzalez is one of those legendary, old-school New York City drink slingers who helped legitimize the bar industry, making bartending a viable career, one perfect classic at a time. His claims to fame include repopularizing the classic Jungle Bird while at Dutch Kills in NYC, and contributing original modern classics such as the Infante to the cocktail canon. But one of Gonzalez's most prized creations, which doesn't get nearly as much love as it should, is the Duke of Suffolk, the signature serve he created for his bar the Suffolk Arms in 2016 (it has since been shuttered).

The cocktail—a blend of gin, English Breakfast and Earl Grey teas, and sugar, topped with whipped cream—is Gonzalez's English take on an Irish coffee–style cocktail. It goes without saying that the recipe shared here is a smaller-format iteration of the modern classic, but like Irish coffee, it goes down well in small portions, to avoid overdoing the caffeine and richness.

ABOUT 2 OUNCES HOT SWEET TEA BLEND (PAGE 111)

¾ OUNCE GIN (SUCH AS LONDON DRY GIN)

LIGHTLY WHIPPED CREAM FOR SERVING

Pour boiling water into a tiny teacup or tempered glass to warm it up. Lightly whip some chilled heavy cream by either shaking in a protein shaker or hand-whisking in a small measuring cup (the consistency shouldn't be runny, but it also shouldn't be thick like fully whipped cream). Meanwhile, heat up the Hot Sweet Tea Blend in a saucepan or in the microwave until hot, but not boiling. Dump the hot water from the teacup and add the Hot Sweet Tea Blend. Pour in the gin. You should have about 1 inch of headroom to layer

CONTINUES

the cream. Give the mix a gentle stir, and float the lightly whipped cream over the drink by pouring the cream over the back of a bar spoon placed just above the liquid.

HOT SWEET TEA BLEND

MAKES 2½ CUPS

1 CUP HOT FRESHLY BREWED ENGLISH BREAKFAST TEA

1 CUP HOT FRESHLY BREWED EARL GREY TEA

1 CUP GRANULATED SUGAR

Combine the teas in a container with a lid, add the sugar, and stir until dissolved. When hot, use immediately for the cocktail. But if kept for later use, store, tightly sealed, in the refrigerator for up to 1 month and reheat 1 serving volume when ready to use.

CAFFÈ DI FORMAGGIO

 Do you remember the Parmesan Espresso Martini that went viral on Instagram in 2023? Well, I may have stoked that fire after covering the infamous martini for *Food & Wine*, resulting in a contentious moment for the magazine in the social media spotlight.

The Caffè di Formaggio—which means "cheesy coffee" in Italian—is an homage to that cheeky serve. But instead of mercilessly shaving parmesan on top of the espresso martini, this sophisticated take serves the cocktail with a side of proper Parmigiano-Reggiano cheese alongside it.

¾ OUNCE VODKA

½ OUNCE BREWED ESPRESSO, CHILLED

½ OUNCE COFFEE LIQUEUR (SUCH AS MR. BLACK)

1 TEASPOON COLD BREW CORDIAL

PARMIGIANO-REGGIANO CHEESE, CUT INTO CHUNKS OR SLICED, FOR SERVING

Garnish: 1 COFFEE BEAN

Pour the vodka, espresso, coffee liqueur, and Cold Brew Cordial into a cocktail shaker with ice and shake vigorously. Double strain into a tiny coupe, garnish with the coffee bean, and serve with the Parmigiano-Reggiano cheese to pair.

↳ COLD BREW CORDIAL

MAKES ABOUT 1⅓ CUP

1 CUP COLD BREW COFFEE

¾ CUP SUGAR

1½ TEASPOONS CITRIC ACID POWDER

Combine the coffee, sugar, and citric acid powder in a microwave-safe container, and heat the mixture for 10 to 15 seconds. Stir until the sugar has dissolved, and set aside to cool to room temperature. Transfer to a bottle and store, tightly sealed, in the refrigerator for up to 1 month.

AUSSIE BREAKFAST

When it comes to mixing mezcal in cocktails, there are a few foolproof flavor pairings, and combining the earthy agave spirit with coffee is one of them. The Aussie Breakfast is designed using the Black Manhattan template—a cocktail made with rye whiskey, Averna amaro, Angostura bitters, and orange bitters. But instead of Averna, I use Mr. Black coffee amaro (a personal favorite from an Australian company that uses coffee liqueur as the base) and a touch of fruit syrup for brightness. It's the perfect serve for imbibers who are just dipping their toes into the world of mezcal.

1 OUNCE MEZCAL

½ OUNCE MR. BLACK COFFEE AMARO

1 BARSPOON MACERATED STRAWBERRY SYRUP

DASH OF ANGOSTURA BITTERS

Garnish: 1 ORANGE PEEL

Combine the mezcal, coffee amaro, and Macerated Strawberry Syrup in a mixing glass with ice and stir to chill and dilute. Strain into a tiny coupe, express the orange peel over the cocktail, and enjoy the drink.

MACERATED STRAWBERRY SYRUP

MAKES ABOUT ½ CUP

1 CUP SLICED FRESH STRAWBERRIES

1 CUP SUGAR

SPLASH OF FRESHLY BOILED WATER

Stir together the sliced strawberries and sugar in a bowl, cover tightly, and set aside to macerate for at least 2 hours, or overnight at room temperature, so the sugar can extract the water content from the strawberries and create a concentrated syrup. Uncover, add a splash of boiled water to dissolve any remaining sugar, and stir to mix. Strain the syrup through a fine-mesh strainer and transfer to a bottle. Store, tightly sealed, in the refrigerator for up to 5 days.

NORDIC COFFEE

Layered shots may not be as popular as they were in the '80s and '90s, but the Hot Shot—a layered balance of Galliano L'Autentico, espresso, and lightly whipped heavy cream—is one of the few that has stood the test of time. Scandinavian folks, in particular, absolutely love the drink, and its undying popularity across the region is one of the main reasons why the Hot Shot is still semi-relevant today. In a way, it's become Scandinavia's answer to Irish coffee—a cocktail that's uplifting and downright delicious, especially during the winter season. I reconstruct this cult favorite shot, transforming it into a drink that closely resembles Irish coffee, except I ditch the whiskey for the Hot Shot's beloved Galliano and split the liqueur with a touch of Nordic aquavit.

½ TO 1 OUNCE HEAVY CREAM, FOR SERVING

¼ OUNCE GALLIANO L'AUTENTICO

¼ OUNCE AQUAVIT (SUCH AS LINIE)

½ OUNCE FRESHLY BREWED ESPRESSO

Pour freshly boiled water into a tiny ceramic or heatproof glass to warm it up. Meanwhile, lightly whip the heavy cream by either shaking in a protein shaker or hand-whisking in a small measuring cup (the consistency shouldn't be runny, but it also shouldn't be thick like fully whipped cream). Dump out the hot water from the cup and pour in the Galliano, aquavit, and espresso. Give the mix a gentle stir, and float the whipped cream over the drink by pouring it over the back of a bar spoon placed just above the cocktail.

MILKING IT

BY **MATT COLVIN**

LAWRENCE PARK
(HUDSON, NEW YORK)

Matt's Milking It is an homage to the early days of Lawrence Park, a bar I had the privilege of helping to open in 2019, and a place that holds a special place in my heart as a result, despite shuttering in 2024. Unlike the simple shooters and boilermakers we offered on the menu when the bar debuted in 2019, this tipple requires a bit more technique to craft what is essentially a clarified Irish coffee, but don't let that deter you. Time is the signature ingredient of this elegant boilermaker. One sip of the popular Left Hand Nitro Milk Stout with this little liquid luxury will surely reinforce that fact. The clarified Irish Coffee batch makes approximately enough for eight small drinks, or two rounds of tiny cocktails for you and three other friends, so crack open a few stouts and enjoy this dessert-like boilermaker in good company.

MAKES 8 TINY COCKTAILS

5 OUNCES IRISH WHISKEY (SUCH AS POWERS)

3 OUNCES COLD BREW CONCENTRATE

2 OUNCES COFFEE LIQUEUR, PREFERABLY ST GEORGE NOLA

2 OUNCES PX (PEDRO XIMÉNEZ) SHERRY

1 OUNCE LEMON JUICE

3 OUNCES WHOLE MILK

STOUT, PREFERABLY LEFT HAND NITRO MILK STOUT, FOR SERVING

Combine the Irish whiskey, cold brew concentrate, coffee liqueur, sherry, and lemon juice in a large measuring cup. Pour the milk into a separate container and slowly pour the cocktail mix into the milk, which will curdle. Seal the container and let it sit for at least 4 hours or refrigerate overnight. To clarify, strain through a superbag or coffee filter. Use immediately or transfer to a clean bottle and store, tightly sealed, in the refrigerator for up to 3 months.

To serve, pour 1½ ounces of the clarified Irish coffee into each chilled tasting glass. Pour about 4 ounces of stout into each small wine glass. Serve both together, so your guests can take a sip of one, then the other, and enjoy accordingly.

THE MISSUS

 Love is memorizing your partner's go-to drink orders. At some point during our relationship, I introduced my wife to the classic Hanky Panky. Since that night, it's become one of her go-to cocktails.

The original Hanky Panky is a Manhattan-style serve with a serious pedigree. It was created at the iconic American Bar at the Savoy Hotel in London, by one of cocktail culture's pioneering female bartenders, Ada Coleman. For the Missus, I don't stray far from the classic recipe, simply swapping the gin with a Chamomile-Infused Gin, which softens the alcohol and adds a comforting floral note reminiscent of having chamomile tea before bed.

¾ OUNCE CHAMOMILE-INFUSED GIN

¾ OUNCE SWEET VERMOUTH

1 BARSPOON FERNET BRANCA

Garnish: 1 ORANGE PEEL

Combine the Chamomile-Infused Gin, vermouth, and Fernet Branca in a mixing glass with ice, stir to chill and dilute, and strain the cocktail into a tiny coupe or martini glass. Express the orange peel over the cocktail, toss it in, and enjoy the drink.

→ **CHAMOMILE-INFUSED GIN**

MAKES 7 OUNCES

1 HEAPING TABLESPOON DRIED CHAMOMILE FLOWERS

7 OUNCES GIN

Combine the chamomile flowers with the gin in a container and let the chamomile infuse the gin for 1 to 2 hours, depending on your preferred strength. Once you're content with the flavor, strain the mixture through a fine-mesh strainer, and transfer to a bottle. Store, tightly sealed, at room temperature. The gin is shelf stable, but is best used within 2 months for optimal freshness.

CHAMOMILE & HONEY TODDY

For this warming, tiny toddy, I employ a split base of an orchard fruit–forward Irish whiskey and the beloved French Pineau des Charentes. The latter is an aperitif from western France made by blending fortified wine from either fresh unfermented grape juice or a blend of lightly fermented grape must with Cognac eau-de-vie. It's this aperitif that gives the Chamomile & Honey Toddy an elegant honeyed sweetness and floral complexity, which is bolstered by the touch of Honey Syrup and softened by the comforting chamomile tea. A tiny serve of this toddy is a creative and quick way to send guests off back into the cold after a lovely food and drink–filled evening, a liquid manifestation of a warm embrace goodbye, if you will.

2 OUNCES FRESHLY BREWED CHAMOMILE TEA

½ OUNCE PINEAU DES CHARENTES, PREFERABLY WHITE

½ OUNCE IRISH WHISKEY, PREFERABLY BUSHMILLS 10 YEAR

¼ OUNCE HONEY SYRUP (PAGE 23)

1 TEASPOON VERJUS

Garnish: 1 THIN LEMON TWIST

Add boiling water to a heatproof ceramic cup or teacup and set aside until the cup is warm. Meanwhile, brew a small cup (enough for two servings) of chamomile tea in a tempered measuring cup (brew according to the tea's packaging). Once the tea has brewed, dump the boiling water from the heated cup. Add the Pineau des Charentes, whiskey, Honey Syrup, verjus, and tea to the warmed cup. Gently stir to blend, and garnish with the lemon twist.

LITTLE

One of the greatest mixology myths is that luxury spirits shouldn't be mixed; rather, they should be savored in their purest form. Ninety-nine percent of the time, this notion is absolutely false. Fine spirits, when mixed with ingenuity and precision, are one of the easiest ways to elevate a simple cocktail. Of course, there are exceptions to this rule, but most of the time, especially if a specific spirit or ingredient can easily be bought again, indulge yourself. This is the essence of what this chapter is all about.

Little luxuries are small-format cocktails that inspire you to mix with fine spirits, fleeting seasonal ingredients, and other more labor-intensive cordials and infusions in applications deserving of their quality and preciousness. Instead of having to painfully pour out a full dose of a fine spirit you'd quite like to enjoy on its own, too, little luxuries allow a bit of liquid sumptuousness to go the distance. These may not be your everyday tiny cocktails, but they're the ideal serves to share with good friends who appreciate life's finest pleasures, to celebrate life with, and to enjoy jubilantly because you only live once.

LUXURIES

CASINO ROYALE

 As an American expat living in London, I'd be remiss not to include a James Bond–inspired cocktail in this book. The Vesper Martini, named after Bond's love interest, double agent Vesper Lynd, first appeared in Ian Fleming's *Casino Royale* in 1953.

My Casino Royale draws the line at shaking the martini—proper martini drinkers would never. Instead, I stir a premium Konik's Tail vodka with a quintessential London dry gin, a pair of vermouths for balanced sweetness, a dash of orange bitters, and a dash of florality and citrus notes from a barspoon of the luxurious Italicus Rosolio di Bergamotto aperitif. Embrace your inner bon vivant and raise a glass to Bond as you enjoy this little luxury.

---

1 OUNCE KONIK'S TAIL VODKA

¼ OUNCE SIPSMITH LONDON DRY GIN

1 BARSPOON DRY VERMOUTH, PREFERABLY NOILLY PRAT

1 BARSPOON BLANC OR BIANCO VERMOUTH, PREFERABLY MANCINO BIANCO VERMOUTH

1 BARSPOON ITALICUS ROSOLIO DI BERGAMOTTO LIQUEUR

DASH OF ORANGE BITTERS

Garnish: 1 LEMON PEEL AND 1 COLD OLIVE

Combine the vodka, gin, vermouths, Italicus, and bitters in a mixing glass with ice and stir until the contents are chilled and diluted. Strain the mixture into a chilled tiny coupe or martini glass. Express the lemon peel over the drink and discard. Garnish with the olive and enjoy.

NOTE: To replicate Wiseman's incredible drink service, also put a small (6½-ounce) carafe in the freezer along with the glasses and batched martinis. When ready to serve, crush 3 cups of ice and put it into a serving bowl large enough for the carafe and garnishes. Nestle the carafe and garnishes in the bowl, and fill the carafe with the batched martinis.

THE BEST FUC$#NG MARTINI SERVICE

BY **CHRISTINE WISEMAN**

BAR LAB HOSPITALITY (MIAMI)

Christine Wiseman is one of those bartenders whose style of hospitality and infectious personality effortlessly convert first-time bar guests into bar regulars. She knows how to read a room and make her guests feel seen and heard—two invaluable traits that every great bartender possesses. Unfortunately, I can't promise that I can convince this bar legend to deliver a pair of tiny silky martinis to you at home. But a recipe from Wiseman that you can easily replicate is the next best thing. She likes her martinis ice-cold, and this style of serving them ensures that every sip is as bracing as the last.

MAKES 2 DRINKS

2½ OUNCES GIN OR VODKA

¼ OUNCE DRY VERMOUTH, PREFERABLY LUSTAU BLANC VERMUT

¼ OUNCE MARTINI RISERVA SPECIALE AMBRATO VERMOUTH

½ OUNCE FILTERED WATER

Garnish: 2 LEMON TWISTS, 4 TO 6 OLIVES, 2 COCKTAIL ONIONS

Combine the gin or vodka, vermouths, and water in a measuring cup and pour into a bottle. Put the batched martinis and two tiny coupes in the freezer to chill for 2 to 4 hours (see Note opposite). After the martini has been chilled, arrange the garnishes on a plate with a few skewers. Take the batched martinis and tiny coupes out of the freezer, and divide the drink between the coupes. Garnish the martini to your liking.

NOTE: You can easily find many kinds of furikake online or in Asian markets.

FURIKAKE SOUR

Furikake—a mixture of sesame seeds, seaweeds, herbs, fish flakes, and salt—was invented in Japan in the twentieth century as a nutritional supplement, commonly served on steamed rice and foods made with rice. It's the ingredient that inspired this approachable vodka-based cocktail, which blends sweet, smoky, and savory flavors in a refreshing sour format. I complement the furikake by using a rice syrup to sweeten the liquid mixture and garnish the drink by rimming the glass with furikake. The result is a bold, silky sour that looks as good as it tastes.

1 LIME WEDGE

½ OUNCE ST. GEORGE GREEN CHILE VODKA

¼ OUNCE EMPIRICAL AYUUK

¼ OUNCE SAKE

2 TEASPOONS LIME JUICE

¼ OUNCE RICE SYRUP

Garnish: FURIKAKE (SEE NOTE)

Sprinkle the furikake on a small plate and garnish a tiny rocks glass or tiny ceramic tumbler: With the lime wedge, wet half the rim of the glass, and dip the wet rim into the furikake. Set aside. Combine the vodka, Ayuuk, sake, lime juice, and Rice Syrup in a cocktail shaker filled with ice and shake vigorously to chill and slightly dilute. Strain into the prepared glass, add a couple ice cubes, and enjoy.

⤷ RICE SYRUP

MAKES ABOUT ¾ CUP

½ CUP RAW WHITE RICE, PREFERABLY A PREMIUM STICKY RICE

½ CUP WATER

½ CUP GRANULATED SUGAR

Combine the rice and water in a small saucepan and simmer for 10 minutes. Remove from the heat, strain out the rice, and return the rice water to the saucepan. Add the sugar and stir until it dissolves. If necessary, put the pan over low heat to help dissolve the sugar. Let the syrup cool to room temperature, transfer to a bottle, and store, tightly sealed, in the refrigerator for up to 2 weeks.

FILTHY BANANATINI

I have a reputation for being obsessed with banana-flavored drinks. When I was bartending at Lawrence Park, in Hudson, New York, I notoriously included Giffard's premium banana liqueur in at least one cocktail per menu. And whenever I was left to my own devices with a "bartender's choice" request, I'd slip in a banana component—tending to the guest's palate preference, of course.

This is a martini-style cocktail that is reminiscent of a banoffee pie—a quintessential British dessert made from bananas, cream, and toffee from boiled condensed milk (or dulce de leche), either on a pastry base or one made from crumbled biscuits and butter. The star of the show is the Mette banana eau-de-vie, a revelation of a specialty spirit, which I first tasted in 2023 at the Gothic Bar, in London, and have been obsessed with ever since. It's a bit pricey, but it's a spirit that you can mix into an array of martinis and also enjoy on its own.

1 OUNCE ALMOND BUTTER–WASHED VODKA (PAGE 134)

½ OUNCE METTE BANANA EAU-DE-VIE

¼ OUNCE DRY VERMOUTH, PREFERABLY BALDORIA

1 HEAPING BARSPOON GIFFARD BANANE DU BRÉSIL

DASH OF ORANGE BITTERS

Garnish: 1 LEMON PEEL

Combine the Almond Butter–Washed Vodka, eau-de-vie, vermouth, banana liqueur, and bitters in a mixing glass filled with ice. Stir to chill and dilute and strain into a chilled tiny coupe. Express the lemon peel over the rim of the glass, discard, and enjoy the cocktail.

CONTINUES

ALMOND BUTTER-WASHED VODKA

MAKES ABOUT 8 OUNCES

8 OUNCES VODKA, PREFERABLY
BELVEDERE LAKE BARTĘŻEK

¼ CUP UNSWEETENED
ALMOND BUTTER, PREFERABLY
ORGANIC

Combine the almond butter and vodka in a zip seal bag (making sure to remove all the air). Fill a saucepan with water and heat it to between 100° and 150°F (below a simmer). Remove from the heat, put the bag in the hot water bath, and infuse the vodka for 3 to 4 hours, reheating the water every 30 minutes or so as it cools. (Alternatively, if you have an immersion circulator, cook sous vide at 120°F for the same length of time.) Remove the bag from the hot water bath and allow it to cool, then freeze for at least 2 hours, or overnight. Strain the contents of the bag through a fine-mesh strainer and then a coffee filter, and transfer to a bottle. Store, tightly sealed, at room temperature for up to 1 month.

> **NOTE:** Try the Almond Butter–Washed Vodka in the Furikake Sour (page 131) as a substitute for the chile vodka.

TNT MARTINY

 When executed with precision, a martini cocktail made with super-premium blanco tequila is a beautiful thing. If you haven't had the pleasure of tasting one yet, then look no further than the savory TNT (tequila and tomato) Martiny.

To up the umami factor, the recipe calls for Tomato Syrup, which can be used in other recipes as well. One sip of this delectable elixir conjures visions of a balcony in Tuscany on a hot summer day, overlooking a bucolic vineyard or farmland, while in front of you sits a plate of tomatoes, fresh herbs, and sliced bread. My hope is that this little luxury transports you someplace just as serene and comforting.

1¼ OUNCES PREMIUM BLANCO TEQUILA, PREFERABLY CASA DRAGONES BLANCO OR PATRÓN EL CIELO

¼ OUNCE DRY VERMOUTH, PREFERABLY NOILLY PRAT

1 TEASPOON TOMATO SYRUP (PAGE 38)

Garnish: BASIL OIL, HOMEMADE (PAGE 137), OR STORE-BOUGHT (OPTIONAL; SEE NOTE), AND 1 SLICE PECORINO CHEESE

Combine the tequila, vermouth, and Tomato Syrup in a mixing glass filled with ice, stir 30 to 35 rotations, and strain into a chilled tiny coupe. Garnish with a few drops of Basil Oil, if using, put the Pecorino in a tiny ramekin, and enjoy.

NOTE: You can buy basil-infused oil online or at specialty grocery stores.

CONTINUES

BASIL OIL

MAKES ABOUT 1 CUP

2 CUPS FRESH BASIL LEAVES

1 CUP PREMIUM EXTRA-VIRGIN
OLIVE OIL

½ TEASPOON COARSE
SEA SALT

Fill a medium pot with water and bring to a boil. Meanwhile, fill a large bowl with water and 1 or 2 cups of ice. Add the basil leaves to the boiling water and blanch for 15 to 20 seconds but no longer, or the basil will lose its vibrant color. Remove the basil from the boiling water with a fine-mesh strainer and immediately plunge the basil into the ice-water bath to stop the cooking and retain the basil's green hue. Let the basil sit in the ice bath for 1 or 2 minutes, remove, and spread them out on a kitchen towel to drain.

Put the blanched basil in a blender, add the olive oil and sea salt, and blend until smooth. Strain the mixture through a fine-mesh strainer lined with cheesecloth, reserving the solids for another use (see Note), and pour into a bottle. Store, tightly sealed, in a cool place until the oil's color is no longer vibrant (approximately 1 to 2 weeks).

NOTE: Use the basil solids in a salad, on a sandwich, or as a garnish on pasta.

UMAMI GIMLET

This bartender-grade drink is a liquid love letter to Chablis, one of my favorite wine regions. To evoke the spirit of Chablis, I reach for Renais gin, made with a base of distilled wine grape skins and lees. I pair this with a funky mushroom cordial and touch of umami vermouth for a unique flavor profile. It may feel easy to write this drink off because of its relative obscurity, but it could launch you on your own flavor-obsessed journey. Don't be afraid to take the leap.

½ OUNCE RENAIS GIN

GENEROUS ¼ OUNCE
MUSHROOM CORDIAL

    ¼ OUNCE DRY
    VERMOUTH,
    PREFERABLY BALDORIA
    UMAMI VERMOUTH

    Garnish: TRUFFLE OIL

Add the gin, Mushroom Cordial, and vermouth to a mixing glass with ice and stir to chill and dilute. Strain up into a chilled tiny coupe or martini glass and garnish with three drops of truffle oil.

→ MUSHROOM CORDIAL

MAKES ABOUT 5½ OUNCES

1 CUP DRIED PORCINI
MUSHROOMS

10 FRESH THYME SPRIGS

1 TEASPOON SEA SALT

7 OUNCES BOILING WATER

1¼ CUPS GRANULATED SUGAR

½ TEASPOON CITRIC ACID
POWDER

In a heatproof measuring cup or bowl, combine the porcini mushrooms, thyme, and salt. Pour in the boiling water, cover, and set aside to infuse for 30 to 60 minutes.

With a fine-mesh strainer, strain the mushroom stock into a saucepan and add the sugar. Heat over low heat, stirring constantly, until the sugar is completely dissolved. Remove from the heat, add the citric acid powder, then let the cordial cool to room temperature. Transfer to a bottle and store, tightly sealed, in the refrigerator for up to 1 month.

NOTE: Once you've mastered this margarita and the Furikake Sour (page 131), give Ayuuk a go in classic Manhattan twists and other marg variations—the uses for this delicious spirit are infinite. And if you want to put a savory twist on the Pasilla Mixe Margarita, substitute Tomato Syrup (page 38) for the agave.

PASILLA MIXE MARGARITA

Ordering a spicy margarita at a bar can be like playing a game of Russian roulette. It took only one throat-charring spicy marg when I was in my early twenties for me to distrust this widely loved twist on the classic Tequila Daisy. Now, as a result of my scarring experiences, I only order the cocktail in bars where I know excruciating pain won't be unintentionally inflicted on me.

To ensure none of my margarita lovers ruin their evenings with a little sip of hellish spice, my Pasilla Mixe Margarita boasts all the earthiness and vegetal notes of the classic without the chile-induced burn, thanks to the Empirical Ayuuk. This chile spirit has subtly sweet and berrylike flavors, but it is dominated by notes of smoked pepper, mole, and nuanced bready characteristics. It marries beautifully with tequila, and it's one of my favorite ways to add vegetal and earthy notes to any cocktail.

Ayuuk is a pricey ingredient, which isn't surprising, given its limited production and high-quality ingredients. But it can easily be enjoyed on its own, as well as mixed into the Furikake Sour (page 131).

¾ OUNCE BLANCO TEQUILA, PREFERABLY TEQUILA OCHO

¼ OUNCE EMPIRICAL AYUUK

½ OUNCE LIME JUICE

1 TEASPOON AGAVE SYRUP (PAGE 23)

1 TEASPOON ORANGE LIQUEUR, PREFERABLY GRAND MARNIER

DASH OF SALINE SOLUTION (PAGE 53) OR A PINCH OF FINE SEA SALT

Add the tequila, Ayuuk, lime juice, Agave Syrup, orange liqueur, and Saline Solution to a cocktail shaker with ice and shake vigorously. Strain up into a chilled tiny coupe and enjoy.

NOTE: You can store the bottle in the freezer, but the mixture can freeze, so keep your freezer between 10 to 14°F if possible. If your freezer is too cold, store in the fridge and freeze before serving. This cocktail is best served with friends.

WET WHITE SHIRT

BY **THIBAULT MASSINA**

LE SYNDICAT (PARIS)

For his tiny cocktail Wet White Shirt, Thibault Massina created a very wet martini that gets the batched-and-chilled-in-the-freezer treatment. This technique gives the spirit-forward serve a luscious mouthfeel and finesse that only the world's best martinis can deliver. According to Massina, the cocktail received its suggestive name because "like a wet white shirt, this cocktail lets the body show through. It gives a classic white shirt another dimension." I like to have mine with some Stilton blue cheese, and I recommend you do the same.

MAKES ABOUT 8 COCKTAILS

11 OUNCES GHEE-WASHED VODKA

2¾ OUNCES PEAR LIQUEUR, PREFERABLY MERLET CRÈME DE POIRE

2¾ OUNCES FINO SHERRY

2¾ OUNCES WATER

Garnish: OLIVES

Combine the Ghee-Washed Vodka, pear liqueur, sherry, and water in a bottle and stir. Freeze for at least 4 hours, but 12 hours is ideal.

To serve, pour 2½ ounces of the ice-cold mix into each chilled brandy snifter or tasting glass, garnish with an olive, and enjoy. If you have leftovers, freeze the bottle for up to 3 months (see Note).

GHEE-WASHED VODKA

MAKES ABOUT 12 OUNCES

12 OUNCES VODKA

5 OUNCES GHEE

Melt the ghee in a saucepan over low heat. Pour it into a 1-quart mason jar or zipseal bag, add the vodka, then let it sit at room temperature while the ghee infuses the vodka for at least 30 minutes. Place the jar in the freezer for 24 hours. Strain the vodka through a fine-mesh strainer and a coffee filter and transfer it to a bottle. The vodka will keep, tightly sealed, in the refrigerator for up to 1 month.

FIG LEAF AND COCONUT WHITE NEGRONI

This twist on the White Negroni lands itself in this chapter because of the seasonality and relative scarcity of fresh fig leaves, depending on where you live. In the United States, fig trees and their fragrant leaves—which express notes of vanilla, coconut, and green walnut—are best foraged in the summer, when the leaves are freshest and full of flavor. The fruit typically ripens and is ready for harvest in the autumn through the end of October.

The grapefruit peel garnish marries beautifully with the coconut aroma, making this appetite-stimulating serve the ideal tiny cocktail to have before dinner on a warm summer's day.

¾ OUNCE COCONUT OIL–WASHED BLANCO TEQUILA (PAGE 146)

½ OUNCE FINO SHERRY

½ OUNCE SUZE GENTIAN APERITIF

1 BARSPOON FIG LEAF CORDIAL (PAGE 146)

Garnish: 1 GRAPEFRUIT PEEL

Put a chunk of clear ice into a tiny rocks glass. Briefly stir the Coconut Oil–Washed Blanco Tequila, sherry, aperitif, and Fig Leaf Cordial in a mixing glass with ice until chilled, and strain over the ice in the rocks glass. Express the grapefruit peel over the cocktail, drop it in the glass for a garnish, and enjoy.

CONTINUES

COCONUT OIL–WASHED BLANCO TEQUILA

MAKES ABOUT 7 OUNCES

8 OUNCES BLANCO TEQUILA

2 OUNCES COCONUT OIL

Combine the tequila and coconut oil in a zipseal bag (making sure to remove all the air). Fill a saucepan with water and heat it to between 100° and 150°F (below a simmer). Remove the pan from the heat, put the bag in the hot water bath, and infuse the tequila for 4 hours, reheating the water bath every 30 minutes or so as it cools. (Alternatively, if you have an immersion circulator, cook sous vide at 120°F for the same length of time.) Remove the bag from the hot water bath and allow it to cool, then freeze until all of the coconut oil has solidified, 2 to 3 hours. Strain the infused tequila through a coffee filter or a strainer lined with cheesecloth and transfer to a bottle. Store, tightly sealed, at room temperature for up to 1 month.

FIG LEAF CORDIAL

MAKES ABOUT 1½ CUPS

1 CUP VERY COLD WATER

1 CUP GRANULATED SUGAR

5 LARGE FRESH FIG LEAVES, SLICED

1½ TEASPOONS CITRIC ACID POWDER

PINCH OF SALT

Combine the water, sugar, fig leaves, citric acid powder, and salt in a blender and pulse to blend until the fig leaves have broken down and imparted a green hue to the cordial, 30 to 60 seconds. Let the blended mixture rest for 1 hour to allow the flavors to marry, stirring once or twice to help the sugar fully dissolve. Strain it through a fine-mesh strainer lined with cheesecloth to remove the fig leaf solids. If the sugar hasn't completely dissolved, add the strained mixture to a saucepan and gently warm it over low heat for a few minutes (avoid bringing the cordial to a simmer). Remove from the heat and let the cordial cool. Transfer to a bottle and store, tightly sealed, in the refrigerator for up to 1 month.

T-PUNCH

In Martinique, a French-speaking island in the Caribbean known for its funky rhum agricole, the locals drink Ti' Punch ("Ti'" being short for *petit*, or "small"). The old-fashioned–style cocktail puts rhum at the forefront, traditionally mixing the spirit with sugar—either a cane syrup or granulated sugar—and a lime peel coin.

Traditionally, the Ti' Punch is served without ice, as it was in the sugarcane fields where it was created. But some contemporary bartenders and tropical cocktail lovers, myself included, break with tradition and dilute their spirit-filled-glass with some cooling ice.

As for the rhum, I reach for Père Labat 59° Rhum Agricole, produced at the historic Distillerie Poisson, located on Marie-Galante, an island off the coast of Guadeloupe. Made from four varieties of heirloom cane indigenous to the pristine Caribbean island, this terroir-driven rum is bottled at a punchy Island Proof (i.e., it has a high alcohol content) and is arguably one of the best examples of rhum agricole in the world. You can also try it in place of Clairin, a Haitian rhum, in the Island Bird (page 151). This cocktail is the Ferrari of rum old-fashioneds, which I shamelessly named after myself.

1½ OUNCES UNAGED RHUM AGRICOLE, PREFERABLY PÈRE LABAT 59° RHUM AGRICOLE

½ OUNCE FINO SHERRY (SUCH AS TIO PEPE)

1 BARSPOON CARIBBEAN COCONUT SYRUP (PAGE 149)

Garnish: 1 LIME PEEL COIN

Put a chunk of clear ice into a chilled tiny rocks glass. Pour the rhum, sherry, and Caribbean Coconut Syrup over the ice in the glass, and stir to chill and add some dilution. Add another small chunk of ice if needed. Express the lime coin over the drink, and then use it to garnish the finished drink.

CONTINUES

CARIBBEAN COCONUT SYRUP

MAKES ABOUT ½ CUP

¼ CUP UNSWEETENED COCONUT FLAKES

1 TABLESPOON ALLSPICE BERRIES

ZEST OF 1 LIME, GRATED

½ CUP CANE SUGAR

⅓ CUP COCONUT WATER, PREFERABLY FRESH

PINCH OF CITRIC ACID POWDER (OPTIONAL)

Put the coconut flakes in a small saucepan and lightly toast over medium-low heat until golden. Remove from the heat and transfer to a small bowl.

Crush the allspice with a muddler and add to the bowl. In the small saucepan you just used, combine the lime zest and sugar. Gently muddle the zest with the sugar to extract the oils, and set it aside for 10 minutes. Finally, add the coconut flakes and allspice mixture, coconut water, and citric acid powder, if using, to the saucepan. Bring to a simmer over medium-low heat, stirring to extract the flavors from the allspice and coconut flakes. When all the sugar has dissolved, remove the syrup from the heat and let it cool in the pan for 30 minutes. Strain the syrup through a fine-mesh strainer lined with cheesecloth, gently squeezing the filtered coconut flakes to maximize yield, and transfer to a bottle. Store, tightly sealed, in the refrigerator for 3 to 4 weeks.

ISLAND BIRD

This twist on the tropical, bittersweet Jungle Bird is another cocktail that was born and bred during my time at Lawrence Park, in Hudson, New York. While the classic Jungle Bird's flavor profile is built around tropical and bittersweet notes, the Island Bird ups the ante with a base of funky rum, which immediately perks up the palate when paired with the abrasively bitter Suze and fresh fruit juices. The rum used in this cocktail is key, as it must be one that's unaged and made from fresh-pressed sugarcane juice (as opposed to molasses) for the cocktail to evoke its signature funkiness.

¾ OUNCE FUNKY UNAGED RUM, PREFERABLY CLAIRIN OR RHUM AGRICOLE

2 TEASPOONS SUZE

¼ OUNCE ACID-ADJUSTED GRAPEFRUIT JUICE (PAGE 62)

½ OUNCE PINEAPPLE JUICE

1 TEASPOON ITALICUS ROSOLIO DI BERGAMOTTO LIQUEUR

1 TEASPOON RICH SIMPLE SYRUP (SEE NOTE, PAGE 22)

Garnish: 1 PINEAPPLE LEAF

Put a small chunk of clear ice into a tiny rocks glass. Combine the rum, Suze, Acid-Adjusted Grapefruit Juice, pineapple juice, Italicus, and Rich Simple Syrup in a cocktail shaker filled with ice and shake vigorously to chill and dilute. Strain over the ice in the rocks glass, garnish with the pineapple leaf, and enjoy.

BABY BROOKLYNITE

"If it ain't broke, don't fix it" pretty much sums up this cocktail, which is a mini version of the Brooklynite. The cocktail is a funky twist on the daiquiri—or Captain's Blood if we're really splitting hairs—to which I was introduced in 2018 at Wm. Farmer and Sons in Hudson, New York, while I was living there.

The key to making this rum sour noteworthy is to make it with a high-ester, or funky, Jamaican rum. Smith & Cross is a popular option, as is the pungent Doctor Bird Jamaican rum, but I prefer Hampden Estate's 8 Year Jamaican rum for the Baby Brooklynite.

---

1 OUNCE HAMPDEN ESTATE 8 YEAR JAMAICAN RUM

SCANT ½ OUNCE FRESHLY SQUEEZED LIME JUICE

SCANT ½ OUNCE HONEY SYRUP (PAGE 23)

DASH OF ANGOSTURA BITTERS

Combine the rum, lime juice, Honey Syrup, and bitters in a cocktail shaker with ice. Shake the mix until it is chilled and diluted, and then double strain the cocktail into a chilled tiny coupe and enjoy.

NOTE: To make the Cacao Nib–Infused Rum, follow the directions for the Cacao Nib–Infused Armagnac on page 105, substituting rum for the Armagnac.

TINY TRIBUTE TO ARHUACA

BY **NAJADE BIJL**

OKURA HOTEL
(AMSTERDAM)

With a round of daiquiris freshly ordered for myself and my mate, I sat at Pulitzer's Bar, in Amsterdam—one of my favorite bars in the world, and the bar where I had my first tiny martini in 2018—watching the young bartender deftly mix drinks. With a cocktail shaker in one hand and two bar spoons held within the other, she shook one drink while simultaneously stirring two others—all while socializing with guests.

It was a swift and subtle display of exceptional technical ability and, considerably impressed, I immediately made Najade Bijl's acquaintance. Her tiny cocktail the Tiny Tribute to Arhuaca, inspired by her visit to Colombia, where the indigenous Arhuaca community taught her about the complexity of cacao, is a sweet and savory cocktail laced with rum, cacao, citrus, and rice. "Maybe it'd be a tad sweet for a lot of people if it were a full-sized drink, but as a tiny cocktail, it's flavor packed and a very refreshing welcome drink with only a hint of chocolate on the finish," says Bijl.

½ OUNCE CACAO NIB-INFUSED RUM, PREFERABLY FOURSQUARE PROBITAS (SEE NOTE)

½ OUNCE RICE SYRUP (PAGE 131)

¼ OUNCE LIME JUICE

SPLASH OF SPARKLING WATER

Garnish: 1 LIME WEDGE

Fill a chilled lowball or similar glass with ice and pour the Cacao Nib–Infused Rum, Rice Syrup, lime juice, and sparkling water over the ice. Gently blend the ingredients by agitating with a bar spoon, garnish with a lime wedge, and enjoy.

BUTTER ME UP

A properly made hot buttered rum is a thing of beauty. A slab of cinnamon-and-nutmeg-infused butter is melted with scalding hot water and mixed with a fortifying measure of aged rum. The butter bit takes some time to prep, but it's all worth it in the end, as its decadence is precisely what the doctor ordered during wintertime.

Butter Me Up reimagines the fussier classic formula to create a version that's easier to make in a small format, once you prep the rum and make the syrup. The herbal Becherovka liqueur lends warming spices, namely ginger and cinnamon, to the tipple, and the drink is made brighter by the Earl Grey tea that features in the syrup. It's a little luxury that warms the soul and is ideal for the end of an evening.

¾ OUNCE BROWN BUTTER-WASHED AGED RUM, PREFERABLY APPLETON 8 YEAR (SEE NOTE)

¼ OUNCE BECHEROVKA LIQUEUR

½ TEASPOON CINNAMON-EARL GREY SYRUP (PAGE 108)

2¼ OUNCES FRESHLY BOILED WATER

Garnish: FRESHLY GRATED NUTMEG

Pour freshly boiled water into a tiny ceramic tumbler or heatproof glass to warm it up. Dump out the hot water, and add the Brown Butter–Washed Aged Rum, Becherovka, Cinnamon–Earl Grey Syrup, and boiled water to the tumbler. Give the mix a gentle stir to blend, garnish with the nutmeg, and enjoy.

NOTE: Follow the recipe for Brown Butter–Washed Calvados (page 167), but substitute aged rum, preferably Appleton 8 Year, for the Calvados.

CHRYSANTHEMUM NO. 2

BY **RUEBEN CLARK**

SILVERLEAF BAR (LONDON)

The Chrysanthemum No. 2 is inspired by one of Clark's favorite classic cocktails, the Chrysanthemum. Fascinated by the classic's peculiar structure, which is 2 parts dry vermouth, 1 part herbal liqueur, and a few dashes of absinthe, Clark adds a twist that leads with the vibrant flavor of Capreolus raspberry eau de vie—a little bit goes a long way with this delightfully potent spirit. This luxurious base is then paired with elderflower liqueur, dry vermouth, and absinthe. Clark notes that a small-format Chrysanthemum is optimal, because it's best served freezing cold. Luckily, that's just the way his tiny drink is served, and it's an extraordinary tipple as a result.

1 OUNCE DRY VERMOUTH, PREFERABLY NOILLY PRAT

½ OUNCE ST. GERMAIN ELDERFLOWER LIQUEUR

¼ TEASPOON CAPREOLUS RASPBERRY EAU DE VIE

2 DROPS ABSINTHE

Briefly stir the vermouth, elderflower liqueur, eau de vie, and absinthe in a mixing glass with ice until chilled. Strain into a chilled tiny coupe and enjoy.

NOTE: The Capreolus raspberry eau de vie is also the perfect after-dinner sipper, or an easy way to add a pop of raspberry to a dry martini—in tiny doses, of course.

BLOWING SMOKE

 I've never been a fan of the classic Manhattan. In 2021, though, I discovered the Rapscallion, a modern classic well known in European bartending circles. It was created by Adeline Shepherd for Ruby, in Copenhagen, back in 2007.

The Blowing Smoke stays true to the Rapscallion's formula, but I up the ante with a pour of the beloved Bowmore 18 Year and a touch of Averna amaro, the latter adding some notes of cola and bitter orange peel, which complement the whiskey beautifully. It's in a league of its own. And no, I'm not just blowing smoke.

ABSINTHE FOR RINSING

1 OUNCE BOWMORE 18 YEAR SCOTCH

¼ OUNCE PX (PEDRO XIMÉNEZ) SHERRY

1 BARSPOON AVERNA AMARO

Garnish: 1 LEMON PEEL AND 1 OLIVE

Pour a dash of absinthe into a chilled tiny coupe or martini glass, rolling it around to coat the glass. Pour out the excess (or drink it). Combine the scotch, sherry, and amaro in a mixing glass with ice and stir until chilled and diluted. Strain the mixture into the tiny coupe, and express the lemon peel over the cocktail and discard it. Garnish the cocktail with the olive and enjoy.

KAIZEN SOUR

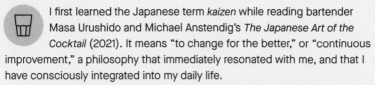 I first learned the Japanese term *kaizen* while reading bartender Masa Urushido and Michael Anstendig's *The Japanese Art of the Cocktail* (2021). It means "to change for the better," or "continuous improvement," a philosophy that immediately resonated with me, and that I have consciously integrated into my daily life.

The Kaizen Sour, a take on Sam Ross's classic Penicillin cocktail, has been one of those drinks that's continuously evolved (for the better) over the years. The final version of this warming whiskey sour has spice, smoke, umami, fresh acidity, and a weighty mouthfeel that makes it a full-on flavor bomb in a tiny glass. Yuzu juice, from an East Asian citrus fruit, doesn't come cheap. But it lends an inimitable mouthfeel and flavor, which makes sourcing it worthwhile. Trying to convert a non–whiskey drinker to whiskey cocktails? Look no further.

1 OUNCE BLENDED SCOTCH, PREFERABLY MONKEY SHOULDER

¼ OUNCE YUZU JUICE (SUCH AS YUZUCO)

¼ OUNCE FRESHLY SQUEEZED LEMON JUICE

¼ OUNCE MISO-HONEY SYRUP (PAGE 77)

1 BARSPOON ANCHO REYES VERDE GREEN CHILE LIQUEUR

1 BARSPOON PEATED SCOTCH

Put a small chunk of clear ice into a chilled tiny rocks glass. Combine the blended scotch, yuzu juice, lemon juice, Miso-Honey Syrup, green chile liqueur, and peated scotch in a cocktail shaker with ice and shake until chilled. Double strain the cocktail over the ice in the glass and enjoy.

LAST CALL

We humans tend to enthusiastically celebrate firsts and lasts, ends and beginnings—occasions when significant memories are formed and, typically, never forgotten. My Pop-Pop wasn't really a whisky drinker in his old age, although I was able to sway him once with a glass of Glenfiddich's fourteen-year-old Scotch whisky, which happened to be the last drink we would share together.

The Last Call, at its core, is a simple take on the Cameron's Kick, an indulgent sour that balances whisky with lemon juice and orgeat, a nut syrup. I position that cherished bottling of Glenfiddich as the cocktail's hero and support it with a jasmine tea–infused Irish whiskey to amp up the drink's floral profile, which pairs well with the Sunflower Seed and Almond Orgeat. The dash of Angostura bitters adds a touch of complexity and cuts through the richness of the drink. I like to think it's another drink I could have persuaded my Pop-Pop to try. It's last call, and this one's for you, sir.

½ OUNCE GLENFIDDICH
14 YEAR SCOTCH WHISKY

¼ OUNCE PREMIUM IRISH
WHISKEY, PREFERABLY
REDBREAST 12 YEAR

¼ OUNCE LEMON JUICE

¼ OUNCE SUNFLOWER SEED
AND ALMOND ORGEAT
(PAGE 88)

DASH OF ANGOSTURA
BITTERS

Combine the scotch, whisky, lemon juice, Sunflower Seed and Almond Orgeat, and bitters in a cocktail shaker with ice. Shake until chilled and diluted, then double strain the cocktail into a tiny coupe or martini glass.

NOTE: If you hate waste as much as I do, save the resolidified brown butter and use for baking or cooking.

FRENCH AF

BY **MOE ALJAFF**

SCHMUCK (NEW YORK CITY)

I met Moe Aljaff while he was still operating Two Schmucks, a bar in Barcelona. It was dubbed the "five-star dive bar," with grungy dive bar vibes but five-star-hotel–caliber service and cocktails.

After parting ways with the bars he founded in 2022, he made the leap across the pond to open Schmuck in New York City, partnering with the unapologetically French Juliette Larrouy, who inspired this caffeinated tiny cocktail. The only detail this little pick-me-up is missing, Aljaff jokes, is a cigarette—then it would truly be a cocktail that's French AF.

---

1 OUNCE BROWN BUTTER-WASHED CALVADOS

    ¼ OUNCE COLD BREW CORDIAL (PAGE 113)

    2 DROPS SALINE SOLUTION (PAGE 53) OR PINCH OF SALT

    Garnish: 1 THIN, TART APPLE SLICE

Put a chunk of clear ice into a tiny rocks glass. Briefly stir the Brown Butter–Washed Calvados, Cold Brew Cordial, and Saline Solution in a mixing glass filled with ice until chilled, and strain the contents over the ice in the glass. Garnish with the apple slice and enjoy.

→ BROWN BUTTER-WASHED CALVADOS

MAKES ABOUT 10 OUNCES

¼ CUP PREMIUM UNSALTED BUTTER (SUCH AS KERRYGOLD)

10 OUNCES CALVADOS

Melt the butter in a saucepan over low heat, stirring constantly to avoid burning it. Once the butter starts to brown and smell nutty, 5 to 8 minutes, remove it from the heat and transfer it to a mason jar. Add the Calvados and whisk. Cool the mixture to room temperature, then freeze until the butter has solidified, about 24 hours. Strain the Calvados through a fine-mesh strainer lined with cheesecloth (see Note) until clear. Transfer to a clean jar and store, tightly sealed, in the refrigerator, for up to 2 weeks.

A WEE IRISH COFFEE

I'll never forget my first Dead Rabbit Irish Coffee (the best in the world, for the record). Ever since that momentous occasion—when I nearly vibrated into the ether from the absurd amount of caffeine and sugar coursing through my body—I've been hooked.

I've spent months—years, even—of my life dissecting the anatomy of an Irish coffee, to understand what makes a perfect one. The quality of ingredients matters, including the freshness of the heavy cream and roast of the coffee beans (preferably until dark or even over-roasted). But I've learned that more than anything, an Irish coffee relies on flawless technique to ensure the drink is balanced and served at its optimal temperature.

My Wee Irish Coffee recipe doesn't reinvent the wheel, but it does call for finer versions of each ingredient for a more luxurious take on the classic. A smaller version is not only ideal for cutting the caffeine but also a good format for ensuring the cocktail retains its heat from start to finish. Follow the directions carefully, and Slàinte mhath! ("Good health!")

---

2 OUNCES FRESHLY BREWED DARK ROAST COFFEE (FOR BEANS ROASTED IN IRELAND, TRY CALENDAR COFFEE)

LIGHTLY WHIPPED HEAVY CREAM, CHILLED, FOR SERVING

¼ OUNCE DEMERARA SYRUP (SEE NOTE, PAGE 22)

½ OUNCE REDBREAST 21 YEAR IRISH WHISKEY

Garnish: FRESHLY GRATED NUTMEG (OPTIONAL)

Pour boiling water into a tiny ceramic tumbler or heatproof glass to warm. Meanwhile, brew the coffee according to the roast's directions, then lightly whip some heavy cream (the consistency shouldn't be runny, but it also shouldn't be thick like fully whipped cream). Dump out the hot water from the glass and pour in the Demerara Syrup, whiskey, and hot coffee. Give the mix a gentle stir, and then float the whipped cream over the drink by pouring it over the back of a bar spoon placed just above the cocktail. Garnish with some freshly grated nutmeg, if you fancy it.

RESOURCES

Not all producers are created equal, and when making cocktails, the quality of the tools, equipment, and ingredients matters. Below are my brand recommendations for various pieces of kit that I suggest throughout the book (mostly in the "Mise en Place" section). While some of these bigger producers are ideal for bar tools and kitchen equipment, when it comes to sourcing glassware and ceramics, I encourage you to research local businesses and artists who are selling bespoke pieces that you can add to your collection. I've found this approach to be the most fulfilling, as each vessel comes with a unique story that will enhance the enjoyment of your cocktail.

Birdy—This is the brand of star bartender Erik Lorincz. It sells stylish and uber-functional bar tools. https://www.birdy-erik.com

Breville—A premium kitchenware company that sells juicers, smoking guns, and other culinary equipment. https://www.breville.com

Cocktail Kingdom—A one-stop shop for everything you need to create bar-quality cocktails at home. https://cocktailkingdom.com

Crew Supply Co.—This producer sells easy-to-clean bottles, which are great for storing infusions and syrups. Their Chubby Bottle is perfect for home use. https://crewsupplyco.com

Ghost Ice System—A premium clear ice mold company, which sells large ice molds for mass production. If you have the freezer space and are keen on having a robust at-home ice program, Ghost Ice may be the answer. https://www.ghosticesystem.com

Kimura Glass Asia—One of the hottest glassware producers in the bar industry at the moment, known for their unique, lightweight designs. https://kimuraglass.com

KitchenAid—A popular company that sells a range of kitchen appliances and tools, including mixers, blenders, and kitchen scales. https://www.kitchenaid.com

MTC Kitchen—A kitchen supply showroom and online retailer specializing in Japanese cooking supplies for both restaurants and home chefs. https://mtckitchen.com

Ninja—This beloved appliance brand is known for its superior blenders and air fryers. https://ninjakitchen.com

Nude Glass—A glassware company that's become the standard for higher-end cocktail bars. The company sells a range of designer glasses at affordable prices. https://us.nudeglass.com

OXO—A tried-and-true brand that sells a range of affordable kitchenware and home bartending equipment. Their Y-peeler and stepped jigger are commonly found in cocktail bars. https://www.oxo.com

Richard Brendon—A British glassware brand that sells luxurious hand-blown glassware. https://richardbrendon.com

Tepotztli—A Mexican brand that sells artisanal bar tools for your home bar. If you're looking for that showstopping piece for your bar cart, look no further. https://www.tepotztli.com

Toyo Sasaki Glass—Japan's largest crystal glassware manufacturer that produces a great range of tiny glasses fit for small-format drinks. https://www.toyo.sasaki.co.jp/e

True Cubes—One of the original clear ice mold companies, which produces good-quality ice molds for clear ice. https://www.truecubes.com

Viski—An alternative site that sells a range of good-quality barware. https://viski.com

Vitamix—The bar and restaurant industry standard for blenders. https://www.vitamix.com/us/en_us

Wintersmiths—A premium clear ice mold company that produces a range of molds for small cubes, 2-inch cubes, ice spears, and ice spheres. https://www.wintersmiths.com

YUZUCO—An American brand that sells bottled yuzu juice as well as superjuice (a more affordable option with yuzu flavor but without the lush mouthfeel). https://www.theyuzu.co

ACKNOWLEDGMENTS

My entire experience writing *Tiny Cocktails*, my first, but hopefully not my last, cocktail book, has been one filled with immense gratitude. Not only for the people who've supported me throughout the publishing process, but for all the editors, friends, family, bartenders, and colleagues who've given me opportunities to flourish in my career as a drinks professional in the last decade. The book is filled with little acknowledgments for these people and places who've impacted me on my journey in the drinks industry. But there are a bunch of individuals who deserve special acknowledgment for their support as I wrote *Tiny Cocktails*.

I must start by thanking Talia Baiocchi, my editor in chief at Punch, who put me forward to Clarkson Potter as a potential author for this book idea. Without Talia's belief in my ability as a drinks writer, I wouldn't be here writing these acknowledgments, so thank you again with the utmost sincerity.

To my wife, and favorite drinking partner, Ailis: Thank you for always pushing me to be the best version of myself and for all of the emotional support you've given me when I've needed it. I love you dearly and relished the chance to express that love in a few tiny cocktails. I promise I'll have more Fernet Branca around the house to make your drink, The Missus (page 121), at a moment's notice.

To my exceptionally kind, thorough, constructive, and enthusiastic editor Deanne Katz: Working with you on *Tiny Cocktails* has been a privilege. Your uplifting support, clear communication, and collaboration has shaped this book into something special. I hope that we have another opportunity to work together in the future. But, until then, it's been a blast (despite all the stress)!

I owe a special thanks to esteemed author and lover of all things amari Brad Thomas Parsons, who kindly put me in touch with David Black Agency when I was exploring options for representation at the start of this journey. This connection led me to Rica Allannic, who I'm honored to have as my literary agent. Thanks for helping me smoothly navigate the business parts of publishing that keep my best interests at heart.

To Eric Medsker, who photographed all of the drinks in *Tiny Cocktails*: I've looked up to your work for many years as a young bartender and photography enthusiast, so to have your images bring my drinks to life is an honor. Thank you so much for taking this project on.

And, last, but not least: Thank you to all the talented bartenders and friends who've contributed recipes to be featured in *Tiny Cocktails*. To have some of your names and works featured in my book is flattering to say the least, and I appreciate the time you all spent submitting recipes. Looking forward to working with you all again in various capacities, and I'll see you on the other side of the bar.

ABOUT THE AUTHOR

TYLER ZIELINSKI is a multidisciplinary drinks professional based in London. In addition to his work in drinks journalism, writing for Punch, *Food & Wine*, *London Evening Standard*, *Eater*, *Condé Nast Traveler*, and other publications, he's also a global bar consultant, content creator, judge, former bartender, and founder of Zest, a content marketing and strategy agency for the bar industry. His entrepreneurial spirit means his work is ever-evolving, but one thing's for certain: A cocktail is always nearby.

INDEX

Published in the United States by
Clarkson Potter/Publishers, an imprint of
the Crown Publishing Group, a division
of Penguin Random House LLC, New York.
ClarksonPotter.com

Library of Congress Cataloging-in-
Publication Data
Names: Zielin, Tyler, author. Title: Tiny
    cocktails / Tyler Zielin. New York :
    Clarkson Potter/Publishers, [2025]
    | Includes index. Identifiers: LCCN
    2024004824 (print) | LCCN 2024004825
    (ebook) | ISBN 9780593796917
    (hardcover) | ISBN 9780593796924
    (ebook) Subjects: LCSH: Cocktails.
    | LCGFT: Cookbooks. Classification:
    LCC TX951 .Z53 2025 (print) | LCC
    TX951 (ebook) | DDC 641.87/4—dc23/
    eng/20240228
LC record available at https://lccn.loc.
    gov/2024004824
LC ebook record available at https://lccn.loc.
    gov/2024004825

ISBN 978-0-593-79691-7
Ebook ISBN 978-0-593-79692-4

Printed in China

Editor: Deanne Katz
Designer: Mia Johnson
Production editor: Ashley Pierce
Production manager: Jessica Heim
Compositor: Merri Ann Morrell
Beverage stylist: Will Blomker
Prop stylist: Maya Rossi
Photo assistant: Randy Smith
Copyeditors: Deborah Kops
    and Alison Kerr Miller
Proofreader: Christina Caruccio
Indexer: Ken DellaPenta
Publicist: Lauren Chung
Marketer: Andrea Portanova

10 9 8 7 6 5 4 3 2 1

First Edition